EXCEL

2019

A Comprehensive Beginners Guide to Learn Excel 2019 Step by Step from A - Z

Introduction

This Excel 2019 Guide gathers all the necessary how-to information on using the different functions of the latest version of Microsoft Excel. Designed in a simple, easy-to-understand language, this book aims to be of service to all users, no matter how much or how little your user experience is with the said program.

As the premier spreadsheet and data analysis application for all kinds of computing devices running under Windows 10, Excel 2019 gives endless capabilities that are often hidden under technical language and masked by explanations that only software engineers and data scientists could decipher. In addition, many of today's how-to guides often present the software's features, but fail to make you realize their specific purpose, or how these features can be of benefit to you.

What's in it for you?

Learning how to use the features offered by Excel 2019 is only the start of the real battle. This book is specially designed not only for you to make use of its functions, but more importantly, to make these features be of use and reap you benefits.

The discussions on this book strike a balance between the "how to" and the "so what" aspects of using Excel 2019. At the same time, it aims to be as clear and simple in its explanations, using a little jargon as possible.

Excel 2019 is worth the learning effort because it is one, if not the best data-processing and analysis applications ever developed. Features such as the Quick Analysis Tool, Flash Fill, Office Add-ins, and Recommended Charts and PivotTables, as well as the Live Preview feature and pre-made galleries allow this version to be the easiest to use. In essence, Excel 2019 is a gold mine to those who rely on the application in their everyday tasks.

About this Book

The Excel 2019 Guide is an all-in reference for Excel users of all levels. And yes, each chapter of this book stands on its own, making it easier for you learn specific features and functions at any time you please.

To find the topic that you want to learn specifically, use the full Table of Contents and Index. You may observe that while the topics are presented in a conversational tone, they are as well direct to the point to foster immediate understanding.

How this Book is Structured

The Excel 2019 Guide is structured in such a way that it can be broken down into smaller, standalone guides that represent specific topics. This is done so in order to speed up the reader's learning process, and as well as to provide laser-targeted representations of Excel's features and functions, as the aim of this book is not to be a mere reference guide, but a power tool to address particular questions as far as the program's features are concerned.

The book is divided into seven integral parts, with each part consisting of two or more chapters that discuss the information needed when working on a certain component of Excel.

Part 1: Excel Basics

This part of the book is intended for those who have not yet had a structured introduction to the basics of Excel. In Chapter 1, you can find an orientation guide to the basic functions and features of the software, in particular how to deal with the popular Ribbon user interface.

This guide also includes a section on touch commands, which can be useful if you happen to be navigating Excel on a touchscreen device such as a smartphone or tablet.

Chapter 2 meanwhile also covers the basics of the software, and it deals with the many ways to customize Excel in accordance to your preferences. It also includes information on personalizing the Quick Access section, and topics on how to use and create add-in programs that further utilize Excel's features.

Part 2: Worksheet Structure

Part 2 discusses the issue of designing Excel worksheets. Chapter 1 under this part focuses on how to create basic worksheet design and covers on the ways of doing data entry, which has become more exciting because of the voice and handwriting input functions.

Chapter 3 talks about how to make your spreadsheet look more formal through formatting. As Excel offers a wide range of formatting techniques, you can go from simple formatting to totally sophisticated presentations and designs.

Chapter 4 covers the ways on how to edit already existing worksheets without distorting design or content. Editing can be gruesome to a new spreadsheet user as most spreadsheets contain not just data entries that you don't want to be disturbed, but also formulas that may destroy the whole worksheet with just a simple mistake.

Chapter 5 of this part briefly discusses how to print spreadsheets. You not only learn how to get raw data to print, but also how to organize them into a professional report your target readers would understand and appreciate.

Part 3: Functions and Formulas

Part 3 of this guide focuses on the calculations and the creation of formulas that produce them. In Chapter 6, you learn about the formal basics, such as doing addition to building an array of formulas using Excel's built-in functions via the Function Wizard. This chapter also talks about how to deal with the different types of cell references and how to link formulas that cover different worksheets.

Meanwhile, Chapter 7 discusses how to prevent formula errors from happening, and how to track them down and get rid of them from your spreadsheet. This chapter likewise talks about circular references in formulas and how you can utilize them for your project.

In Chapters 8 to 10, you learn how to make use of the different kinds of built-in functions, from calculating elapsed time, financial functions to reveal and identify monetary-related computations, math and statistical functions, and as well as lookup, information, and text functions.

These chapters help build formulas that automate data entry and by reverting values from a source lookup table, get the lowdown on any chosen cell in the worksheet, and merge your chosen pieces of text.

Part 4: Worksheet Review and Collaboration

In Part 4, you learn at the different ways in which you can share your spreadsheet data to others. These include how to protect your data and provide viewing and editing permissions to other users on Chapter 11, and building and using hyperlinks in Excel spreadsheets in Chapter 12. Also in this chapter are ways to build hyperlinks that can be used to move from worksheet to worksheet within the same file, opening documents, or connecting to the internet.

Meanwhile, Chapter 13 talks about Excel's features to send out spreadsheets and allowing people to review and comment on them. It also includes ways to review and reconcile suggested changes made on your worksheet.

Chapter 14 discusses sharing spreadsheet data with other programs, most especially on other Office 2019 programs. This chapter likewise talks about the ways to share workbooks online, from inviting people to view or co-author them, to attaching them to email messages, and adding comments as a portable document format (PDF) file via the AdobePDF add-in.

Part 5: Graphics and Charts

In Part 15, you will learn how to use the graphical aspects of Excel. In Chapter 1, you are taught how to chart spreadsheet data. Excel 2019 has functions to create awesome charts, which you can do by selecting the right type of chart or graph for your data that you want to present.

Chapter 16 of Part 5 talks about other graphics that can be added on your spreadsheets. These include graphic objects that can be drawn and imported, such as clip art included in the MS Office package, and digital images created using other hardware and software.

Part 6: Data Management

In Part 6, you will learn the ins and outs of using Excel to keep large amounts of data in databases. Chapter 17 introduces you to the basics of how to set up a database and how to add your data to your list. In this chapter you will also find information on how to organize data by sorting and how to add up its numerical data using the Subtotal function.

Chapter 18 on the other hand talks about filtering data and extracting specific information, also known as querying. In this chapter, you'll discover how to do different filtering operations, from using the AutoFilter feature to doing custom filters and specialized database actions. Likewise, this chapter offers a quick look at automating tasks on Excel by using macros and the Visual Basic Editor.

Part 7: Data Analysis

In this part of the book, you are introduced to the subject of data analysis using Excel. You are taught how to use the software's computational features to project and predict future outcomes.

In Chapter 19, you get to see the different ways to do what-if scenarios, such as one and two-input variable data tables, performing goal seeking, setting a series of different scenarios, and making use of the Solver add-in.

Chapter 20 meanwhile discusses creating special data summaries known as pivot tables which allow you to analyze larger amounts of data in a compact and changeable format. In this chapter, you learn how to create and control pivot tables and build charts that depict summary information in a graphic manner. You also learn how to use 3D Maps and ForeCast Sheet features in order to create sophisticated kinds of data analysis on the data model on your Excel pivot table.

Navigating through this Book

The discussions in this book are inspired by Microsoft's online articles and help references. If you may notice, the topics follow the sequence of the Ribbon command and short or hotkeys that you encounter in the application.

Excel 2019 follows the Ribbon Interface which was first introduced to users in Excel 2007. This is explained in Part 1, Chapter 1, so as to make you more comfortable with its command structure. With this as the starting point, it will be easier for you to navigate through the book's chapters, as many of its discussions begin with Ribbon command sequences.

To further appreciate this book, you are encouraged to type something into a specific cell in your Excel worksheet. This is not only a means to test the functions being discussed, but to give you a first-hand experience in using Excel for your needs.

Using Excel can be overwhelming, especially to those who do not make use of its features and functions on a regular basis. But at some point in your life, you have to deal with data and its need to be contained, controlled, and managed. While Excel 2019 already offers a lot of methods to make data management much easier, this book meanwhile enables you to get the most of its features for you to enjoy.

PART 1:

<u>The Basics of Excel</u>

Chapter 1

The Basics of Excel 2019

What to expect from this chapter?

- Get acquainted with Excel 2019's Start screen and program window
- Choosing commands from the Ribbon
- Removing the Ribbon
- How to use Excel 2019 on a touchscreen device
- Navigating the worksheet and workbook
- The "Tell Me" feature
- Opening and closing Excel

Just like its predecessors beginning from 2007, Excel 2019 has been reliant on the Ribbon, and this means you can select the majority of the Excel commands on this area. It likewise has the Quick Access Toolbar, and the Quick Analysis tool and mini-bar that can be used for context-sensitive functions and commands. It also provides task panes such as Research, Clipboard, Thesaurus, and Selection, among others.

Excel 2019 has features that support certain style and formatting functions, similar to MS Word and MS PowerPoint, such as the Live Preview, that allows you to see how your actual worksheet data appears using a particular style, before you apply it. Excel also has the Page Layout feature, which displays rulers and margins together with the headers and footers for each worksheet. It also has a zoom slider that allows users to zoom in and zoom out on the data.

Meanwhile, the Backstage view that can be located at the File tab on the Excel Ribbon allows you to get an at-a-glance information about your spreadsheet files, and do functions such as preview, save, share, and print.

The Excel 2019 also has various pop-up galleries that allow formatting and charting easier, and these can all be done also on the Live Preview function.

Excel 2019's New Look and Feel

One of the most striking format developments in Excel 2019 is that its user interface is flatter and more towards the monochromatic side (simply put, from 3-D to 2-D, from multicolor to monotone).

Yes, the contoured command buttons and the colorful Ribbon and pull-down menus and gradients are no longer present, in contrast to the previous versions. Shading is reserved only for the rows and columns being selected on the worksheet.

This look and feel are not only observed on Excel 2019, but for all Office 2019 applications, and is due to the Windows 10 user experience. This version of the Windows operating system was developed for a smoother work across different devices, from desktop to laptop to smartphones to tablets, as well as devices with smaller screen sizes and where touch is the primary means of selecting and controlling screen objects.

Through this perspective, Microsoft remodeled the interface of its operating system and Office 2019 applications. It tried to reduce the complexity of various screen elements and make them as responsive as they can on touchscreen devices.

The result of this a snappy, smart Excel 2019, which works well on any hardware to which it is installed. Despite the plainer look, this version of Excel boasts a faster, more efficient functionality.

Perhaps the best thing about the current look of Office 2019 is that each of its application programs offers a different base color. Excel 2019 features a green color scheme which is applied all throughout its screen elements from the Status bar, cell outline pointer, shading of the highlighted and selected Ribbon tabs all the way up to Excel's program and file icon,.

The Excel Start Screen

When you open Excel 2019, the program welcomes you with a Start screen. This screen is primarily divided into two panes, the left green navigation pane with the Home icon and contains New and Open items at the top, while the buttons about Account, Feedback, and Options are placed at the bottom.

The right pane meanwhile displays a single row of thumbnail containing different templates that can be used to launch a new workbook, with a list of some of the most recently opened workbooks. To find more templates, you may click the "Find More in New Link" option on the right side of the Home screen, or the New icon located in the left part of the navigation pane.

To launch an existing Excel workbook that is not displayed on the Recent list, click the "Find More in Open" link.

The first template you will see on the top row of the Home tab is called "Blank Workbook," and you may choose this thumbnail to begin a new spreadsheet of your own design. The second thumbnail to called "Welcome to Excel," in which you can open a workbook with 10 worksheets; this enables you to go on a tour and play around with the different features of Excel 2019.

When you click the "Create" button after clicking this thumbnail, the program opens a new "Welcome to Excel1" workbook, where you can practice with it using the Flash Fill feature to fill a series of data entries. The Quick Analysis tool meanwhile gives a preview of the formatting, totals, charts, and pivot tables and spark lines that you can add to the table of data.

Once you are done experimenting with these basic features, you may close the workbook by selecting File and going to Close, or pressing the Ctrl+W hotkey and then choosing the "Don't Save" button in the alert pop-out dialog box.

If there are no Excel templates displayed in the Home screen that fits the bill, then click "Find More in New Link" to select New in the Navigation pane and display the New screen that displays a new array of standard templates that you can choose to use for new and succeeding worksheets. These templates include those that can be used for tracking projects, creating invoices, and making calendars, among others.

The Ribbon User Interface

When you open a new blank workbook by clicking the New Workbook thumbnail in the Home screen, Excel 2019 displays a single worksheet (under the generic name, Sheet1) via a new workbook file (with the filename Book1) inside a program window.

The Excel window containing this worksheet of the workbook is composed of the following:

- File menu button – when clicked, program opens the Backstage view, where you can find a set of file-related options such as Info, New, Open, Save, Save As, Print, Share, Export, Publish, Close, and Account. You will also find the Options button, which allows you to change Excel's default settings.

- Quick Access toolbar -this consists of AutoSave, Save, Undo, and Redo functions. AutoSave is engaged after you manually save a workbook to OneDrive or SharePoint. Meanwhile, you can click Save, Undo, and Redo buttons to do tasks to save your workbook for the first time and save changes when AutoSave is not engaged, as well as undo or redo changes. You may likewise click the Customize Quick Access Toolbar to open a drop-down menu that has additional common functions such as New, Open, Quick Print, etc.

- Ribbon – most of Excel's commands are found on the Ribbon, and are arranged into a series of tabs beginning from Home to View.

- Formula bar – this shows the address of the current cell together with its contents.

- Worksheet area – this area contains the cells of the present worksheet and are identified by column headings that use letters along the top, and row headings that use numbers. To move around the worksheet, use the horizontal and vertical scroll bars.

- Status bar – this bar gives you the information about the program's present mode and the keys you engage. It allows you to choose a new worksheet view and to zoom in or out of the worksheet.

When you are using Excel 2019 on a touchscreen gadget, the Ribbon display options are set to Tabs (so that the currently engaged commands appear only when you lick a tab). To make navigation easier using a finger or stylus, you can add the Touch/Mouse mode button to the Quick Access toolbar and engage touch mode by tapping the Customize Quick Access Toolbar button before tapping the Touch/Mouse Mode option on the drop-down menu.

With the touch mode on, Excel shows its drop-down menu and the command buttons on the Ribbon. This way, you have a better chance of correcting selecting functions with your finger or stylus. Meanwhile, on a table such as the Microsoft Surface Pro, Excel automatically adds a Draw tab to the Ribbon that contains various inking options that allow you to change settings for drawing with your finger, stylus, or Surface Pen.

Exploring Excel's Backstage view

Just below the AutoSave button, you can find the File menu button. When you click the File menu button or press Alt + F, the Excel Backstage view appears together with the Home screen. In this view, you can find a menu of file-related options on a column on the left side, and, depending on which option selected, panels containing at-a-glance information and other command options can be found.

At first, the File menu button may seem like a Ribbon tab. However, keep in mind that once you click this, it automatically leads to a totally new non-worksheet screen with the Backstage view. This screen has its own options but has no Ribbon-related commands.

Once you click the File menu button to go to the Backstage view, you can click the Back button that is displayed above the Info menu to go back to the normal worksheet view. You may also press the Esc key.

Getting to know the Info screen

When clicking File ⇒ Info in the Backstage view, an Info screen appears. On the left of the Info screen, you find the following commands:

- Protect Workbook –to encrypt the Excel workbook file with special access, such as a password, protect its contents, or verify contents of the file using a digital signature.

- Inspect Workbook –to check the document for metadata (data about the file) and see the file's access options for people with disabilities and compatibility with earlier Excel versions.

- Manage Workbook –to recover or delete draft versions that are saved via AutoRecover

- Browser View Options –to manage parts of the Excel workbook that can be viewed or edited by users

- Properties –lists the size of the file as well as if there is any other info such as Title, Tags, or Categories dedicated to it. To add or edit this info, click the appropriate text box and start typing. To change additional file properties, you may click the Properties drop-down menu and click Show Document Panel from its drop-down menu.

- Related Dates –lists the date the file was in terms of Created, Last Modified, and Last Printed.

- Related People –lists names of the workbook's author and other persons who last modified the file.

- The Show All Properties link –when clicked this expands the list of properties such as Comments, Template, Status, Subject, Categories, Hyperlink Base, and Company that can be edited.

Other File Menu options

On top of the Info option at the File menu, you can find the commands that you use to work with on Excel workbook files. These include creating new workbook files and opening existing workbooks for editing.

Below the Info option, you find the Save and Save As commands. You use the Save command to save changes made to a workbook, while the Save As command saves changes under a new filename or in a new location on your computer or Cloud.

Under the Save As command, you find the Print option which, when chosen, shows a Print screen. This screen offers the document's current print settings on the left and a preview area on the right.

Also below the Print command is the Share option, which displays a list of functions that allow you to share your workbook files online. You will also find an Export option that I used to open the Export screen. In this screen you will find options on how to convert workbooks to other file types. The Publish option on the other hand enables you to save Excel workbooks to a folder on OneDrive and then publish them to Microsoft's Power BI (Business Information) stand-alone application that allows you to create visual representations that show and explain the story behind your worksheet data.

Checking user and product information

Below the Close option on the File Menu, you will find the Account option. You may use this option to check account-related information on the Backstage Account screen. When shown, the Account screen gives you both product and user info.

On the left of this screen you will find user information, which includes all online services that you are currently connected, such as social media sites, and corporate services like OneDrive, SharePoint, and Office 365.

To add an online service to the list, just click Add a Service button at the bottom and choose the service to add on the Image and Videos, Storage, and Sharing continuation menus. To control which accounts to appear on the list, select the name and click the Remove button to get it off the list, or click the Manage button then edit the settings.

On the right of the Account screen, you will find the Subscription Product Information. In this section you can see the activation status of your MS Office programs and review the version of Excel that is running on your device. Since many Office 365 licenses allow up to five installations on different devices, you may click Manage Account to take you online. You can check how many installations you have available, and manage the devices wherein Office 2019 is activated. If you need more installations, you may use the Change License button to upgrade to another subscription plan.

Ripping through the Ribbon

The Ribbon groups relevant commands together so that you become familiar with all the most commonly used commands and options to perform certain Excel tasks.

The ribbon consists of the following sections:

- Tabs – Excel's main tasks are grouped together and show all commands needed to perform a core task.

- Groups – Related commands that can be organized into subtasks that are often performed as part of the tab's bigger core task.

- Command buttons – In each group you can find command buttons that you may click to do a certain action or open a gallery.

- Dialog Box launcher – This button is found on the lower-right corner of certain groups, and it leads to a dialog box with another set of additional options that you can use.

To learn more of the Worksheet area displayed in the program window, you can minimize the Ribbon so that only the tabs are seen, and this is more ideal when working on a touchscreen device. When the Ribbon is pinned to the Excel screen, you can minimize it via the following steps:

1. Click the Collapse the Ribbon button

2. Double-click the Ribbon tab

3. Press Ctrl+F1

4. Right-click and click the Collapse the Ribbon option at the drop-down menu

To display the entire Ribbon together with its command buttons in the program window, then click the selected tab and then click the Pin the Ribbon button. You may also do this by pressing Ctrl+F1 again.

When working n Excel with the Ribbon minimized, keep in mind that the Ribbon expands every time you click any of its tabs to see its command buttons, but this tab only stays until you click any of its command buttons. Excel automatically minimizes the Ribbon to allow only the tabs for display.

On keeping the tabs

When you first launch Excel 2019 and open a workbook, the Ribbon has seven tabs, and these are:

- Home – This tab is used to create, format, and edit a spreadsheet. It is arranged into the Font, Clipboard, Alignment, Number, Styles, Cells, and Editing options.

- Insert – This tab is used to add particular elements to a spreadsheet. It is set via Tables, Illustrations, Apps, Charts, Reports, Sparklines, Filter, Links, Text, and Symbol groups.

- Page Layout – This tab is used to prepare a spreadsheet for reordering graphics or printing. You can use its options such as Themes, Page Setup, Scale to Fit, Sheet Options, and Arrange.

- Formulas – This tab is used when adding formulas and functions to your spreadsheet. This can also be used to check formula errors. It is arranged into Function Library, Defined Names, Formula Auditing, and Calculation groups. This tab also has a Solutions group to activated certain add-in programs, including Conditional Sum and Euro Currency tools.

- Data – This tab can be used for importing, outlining, querying, and subtotalling data in a worksheet. This tab is arranged into the following groups: Get External Data, Connections, Sort and Filter, Data Tools, and Outline.

- Review – this tab is used for proofing, marking up, and protecting a worksheet for others to review. This tab is grouped into several options, such as Proofing, Language, Comments, Changes, and Ink.

- View – this tab is used when editing or changing the display of the Worksheet area and that data it carries. You may use its options such as Workbook Views, Show, Zoom, Window, and Macros.

- Help – this tab is used to get help online and for training on using Excel.

If you are using Excel 2019 on a touchscreen device, you will also see the Draw tab on your Ribbon. The Draw tab enables you to change inking options when using a drawing device.

While these mentioned tabs are the standard on the Ribbon, they are not the only tabs that may be seen in this section. Excel also shows contextual tools with their own tab, and the name of the tab appears above the tab or tabs related to the tools.

Once you deselect the object, the contextual tool for that specific object and all of its related tabs also disappear from the Ribbon, leaving the regular tabs displayed.

The Developer Tab

If you happen to be doing a lot of work with macros and XML files on Excel, then you should as well add the Developer tab to the Ribbon. This tab has all the necessary buttons used to create, play, and edit macros and import XML files. To do this, you can follow these steps:

1. Click the File menu, followed by Options on the Backstage view.

2. Click the Customize Ribbon (ALT+FTC).

3. Click the Developer check box under the Main Tabs in the Customize the Ribbon list, then Click OK to finish.

Selecting using keyboard and mouse

since Excel 2019 runs on different devices, the best means of selecting Ribbon commands is based on the device and as well as the way the device is equipped.

The best direct method to select Ribbon commands using a physical keyboard and mouse is to click the tab that contains the said command button and clicking the button in its groupset. For example, if you want to place an online image onto your spreadsheet, you should click the Insert tab and then click Online Pictures to see the Online Pictures dialog box.

The easiest way to choose commands on the Ribbon is to press the Alt key and then the letter of the hotkey that appears on the tab you wish to select. Excel then shows all the command button hotkeys next to their corresponding buttons, along with the hotkeys for Dialog Box Launchers.

Selecting Ribbon commands by touch

Meanwhile, when you select Ribbon commands on a touchscreen device, you are limited to choosing them directly by touch.

You can do this by first turning on the Touch/Mouse Mode button. Excel then spreads the command buttons by adding more space around them, so that you can actually choose the command by tapping your finger right next to it.

Using the Formula Bar

The Formula Bar shows the cell address and the items contained in the said cell. The address of the cell is identified by its column letter followed by the row number. It begins with cell A1 and ends in cell XFD1048576.

The Formula Bar has three parts, namely:

- Name box – the leftmost section that displays the address of the cell.

- Formula bar buttons – the middle section that displays only an indented circle with the Insert Function Button (fx) on the right, or until you edit a cell entry.

- Cell contents – the third section takes up the rest of the bar and expands to display long cell entries that won't fit in the normal area.

The Cell contents section is really important because it shows the contents of the cell even when the worksheet does not. The contents of the cell are completely editable. Likewise, when the Cell contents area is blank, it means that it is empty.

The Worksheet Area

The Worksheet area is where the Excel action takes place, as it displays the cells in different sections and parts of the worksheet. You do all the data entry and formatting in this area, as well as all the editing. Do remember that for you to enter and edit data, the cell must be current. Excel identifies a current cell by: (a) the green border surrounding the cell appears in the cell, (b) the cell address appears in the Name box of the Formula bar, (c) the current cell's column letter and row number are shaded in the column and row headings.

Navigating the worksheet

Excel offers many ways to move around the worksheet so you can enter new data or edit existing data. These include clicking the desired cell, clicking the Name box and typing the address of the desired cell and then pressing the Enter key, pressing Alt+HFDG, Ctrl+G, or F5 to open the Go To dialog box and typing the address of the desired cell and then clicking OK, and using the cursor keys, using the horizontal and vertical scroll bars of the Worksheet area to move the portion of the worksheet that contains the intended cell.

Each new workbook contains a single blank worksheet, named Sheet1, and it contains 16,384 columns and 1,048,576 rows. If you still need more worksheets, you can add by clicking the New Sheet button. On the left side of the bottom part of the Worksheet area is the Sheet tab scroll buttons, followed by the tabs for the worksheets. To activate, select it by clicking the sheet tab.

Help

Help is available in two ways: the Tell Me feature and Online Help. The Tell Me feature is a text box located at the immediate right of the last tab of the Excel ribbon. You can enter a topic and Excel displays a list of relevant commands via a drop-down list. When you choose one of the items on the list, Excel either chooses the associated Ribbon command and waits until you select from the command's submenu or completes the associated command sequence.

Getting Help from the Help Tab

Excel 2019 also offers online help in the Help taskbar. To display this, you just click the Help button or Alt+Y2H or press F1. Once you do this, an Excel 2019 Help task pane appears.

Starting and Leaving Excel

Since Windows 10 brings back the Start menu, you can click the Start menu button and search for the Excel 2019 item and icon for the program to launch.

On the other hand, if you are about to leave Excel, you can do so via either of the following actions: (1) press Alt+FX or Alt+F4; (2) select the Close button in the upper right hand corner of the program; (3) right click the Excel program window to close the workbook file, (4) or right-click the Excel program icon on the Windows 10 taskbar then click the Close Window(s) option on the pop-up menu.

If you exit Excel and have not yet saved the latest changes on your workbook, the program will display an alert message asking whether you want to save these. To save before exiting, click the Yes button; if you don't want to save the changes you've made, then click the No button.

Chapter 2

Personalizing Your Excel 2019

What to expect from this chapter?

- How to customize the Quick Access toolbar
- Changing Excel's program settings
- Extending Excel capabilities via add-ins

Personalizing the Quick Access Toolbar

Excel offers a wide array of ways for it to be personalized in accordance to your needs and usage preference. You can customize your Excel program in three ways, via the (1) Quick Access toolbar, (2) making modifications to the default settings, and (3) add-ins.

Tailor-fitting the Quick Access Toolbar

In Excel 2019, you are able to make changes to the Quick Access toolbar, which appears on the left side of the screen just above the Ribbon. It has four command buttons: AutoSave, Save, Undo, and Redo.

Meanwhile, if you want to add other commands that you often use, just click the Customize Quick Access toolbar button and then click the command to be added to the toolbar.

If you want to add Ribbon commands to the Quick Access toolbar, you can do so by right-clicking a Ribbon command button on the Ribbon and then click Add to Quick Access Toolbar from the shortcut menu. Excel will immediately add the said button to the end of the toolbar.

If you wish to move the command button to another location within the Quick Access toolbar, you have to click the Customize Quick Access toolbar button and then click More Commands from the drop-down menu.

Adding non-Ribbon commands

You may also add other options on the Quick Access Toolbar tab even if they are not on the Ribbon. You can do so through the following steps:

1. Select the type of command you are going to add, such as Popular Commands, Commands not in the Ribbon, All Commands, and Macros, among others.

2. Click the command option that you want to add to the Quick Access Toolbar in the Choose Commands From list box on your left;

3. Click the Add button to include the chosen command button to the bottom of the list box on your right.

4. Click OK to close the dialog box.

Exploring your Options

Whenever you open a new workbook, Excel creates assumptions on how you want your spreadsheet and chart information to appear both on screen and print. These assumptions may not always fit your preferences. Hence it is important that you know how to explore the Options the program offers for you to maximize Excel's features.

User Interface Options

The User Interface Options contain the following boxes and buttons:

- Using Multiple Displays —enables you to choose the Optimize for Compatibility, so you can enjoy Excel plus the other windows you have on connected display screens look their best.

- Show Mini Toolbar – disables and reenables display of the mini-toolbar that contains the most important formatting Home Tab buttons.

- Show Quick Analysis Options – disables or reenables the appearance of the Quick Access toolbar.

- Enable Live Preview – enables or disables the Live Preview feature.

- ScreenTip Style – changes the way ScreenTips information is displayed.

When Creating New Workbooks

You will find this group in the Popular tab of the Excel Options dialog box, and it includes four combo and text boxes:

- Use This as the Default Font – to choose a new default font to use on all cells of worksheets by entering the font name in the combo box.

- Font Size – to choose a new default size on all worksheets.

- Default View for New Sheets – you can select either Page Break Preview or Page Layout as the default view for all new worksheets.

- Include This Many Sheets – add or reduce the default number of worksheets in a new workbook (you can enter a number between 2 and 225).

Personalize Your Copy of Microsoft Office

This section contains three options:

- Username – this text box allows you to change the username being used as the author for new workbooks created in Excel 2019.

- Office Background – this contains a drop-down menu that allows you to choose a background pattern to be displayed on the right side of the program where your information, Ribbon Display Options, and Minimize, Restore and Close buttons are located.

- Office Theme – this drop-down menu allows you to choose different tint options – Colorful, Light Gray, and White.

Start-Up Options

The Start-Up Options contain the following selections:

- Choosing Extensions You Want Excel to Open by Default – when you open the Default Programs button, you will see a Set Associations for the Program dialog box that allows you to choose the types of application files that you want to be associated with the program.

Double click any file carrying the chosen extension to launch Excel 2019.

- Tell Me if Microsoft Excel Isn't the Default Program for Viewing/Editing Spreadsheets – this box determines if you are informed or not should another Spreadsheet program or viewer be associated with Excel workbook files.

- Show the Start Screen When the Application Starts – This box determines if the Start screen appears whenever you launch Excel 2019;

Calculation Options

The Calculation Options allow you to edit when formulas in your workbook are recalculated, and how a formula that Excel cannot solve on the first try can be recomputed. You can choose from the following items:

- Automatic – makes Excel recalculate all formulas after you modify any of the values that are dependent on their calculation.

- Automatic Except for Data Tables – makes Excel recalculate formulas except for those entered into the What-if data tables. To update formulas, click Calculate

Now (F9) or the Calculate Sheet (Shift +F9) button on the Formulas tab.

- Manual – this option button switches to total manual recalculation, so formulas that need updating are recomputed only when you click Calculate Now or the Calculate Sheet commands.

- Enable Iterative Calculation – this checkbox enables or disables iterative calculations for formulas Excel couldn't solve on its first try.

- Maximum Iterations – the text box to change the number of times Excel recalculates an insolvable formula.

- Maximum Change – this text box is used to change the amount by which Excel increases its guess value that it applies when recalculating a formula in the attempt to solve it.

Working with Formulas Options

Working with Formulas Options has four checkboxes containing formula-related options:

- R1C1 Reference Style – this checkbox enables or disables the R1C1 cell reference system where columns and rows are numbered as R45C2 for cell B45.

- Formula AutoComplete – disables or re-enables the Formula AutoComplete feature where Excel tries to complete the formula or function that you are manually editing.

- User Table Names in Formulas – to disable and re-enable the feature where Excel applies range names you have created in a table of data.

- Use GetPivotData Functions for PivotTable References – this disables or re-enables the GetPivotTable function that Excel uses to get data from various fields in a data source.

Error Checking and Error Checking Rules

The other options on the Formulas tab of the Options dialog allow you to manage error-checking for formulas.

In the Error Checking option, the only check box is Enable Background Error Checking, which allows you to do error-checking in the background while you are doing other Excel tasks.

The Error Checking Rules, check an indicated formula error when a formula refers to an empty cell.

Data Options

The Data Options under the Data tab contains four check boxes. These options allow you to control the way Excel handles huge amounts of data that you can access through external data queries, or through Excel's pivot table feature.

Excel 2019 disables the undo feature when refreshing data in a pivot table from external data that has 300,000 or more source data. To modify the minimum number of source rows, enter a new number in the text box that contains the default value of 300 under the Disable Undo for Large PivotTable Refresh Operations check box.

For all refresh operations in large pivot tables, just deselect the Disable Undo for Large PivotTable Refresh Operations check box.

Excel 2019 disables by default the Undo feature for Excel data lists that are made from related external database tables that are more than 64MB. To change this, enter a new number in the text box containing the default value of 64.

To enable the Undo feature for all operations involving data lists, just deselect the Disable Undo for Large Data Model Operations box.

AutoCorrect Options

The AutoCorrect Options dialog box has four tabs:

- AutoCorrect – controls which corrections Excel automatically makes.

- AutoFormat As You Type – check box options that control whether or not to replace Internet addresses and network paths with hyperlinks.

- Actions – with an enable Additional Actions, let you activate a date or financial symbol context menu that appears when you fill in a certain date or financial text in the cells.

- Math AutoCorrect – using Replace and With text box that allows you to replace the certain text with math symbols needed on your worksheet.

Modifying Save Options on the Save Tab

There are four sections under the options of the Save tab, and these are:

- Save Workbooks,

- AutoRecover, Exceptions for the current workbook

- Offline Editing Options for Document Management Server Files

- Preserve Visual Appearance of the Workbook

Customizing the Excel 2019 Ribbon

The options under the Customize Ribbon tab of Excel Options allow you to change which tabs appear on the Excel Ribbon and the order they appear, and to edit which groups of command buttons can be seen on each of the tabs. You can also use these options to create new tabs for the Ribbon and create custom groups of command buttons within the displayed tabs.

Customizing Ribbon tabs

If you want the default arrangement of the main tabs and groups on the Excel Ribbon to be modified according to your liking, you can do so by the following actions:

- Hide tabs on the Ribbon – deselect their check boxes in the Main Tabs list box on the right side of the Excel Options.

- Modify tab order on the Ribbon – select the tab to move and then click Move Up or Move Down until the name of the tab appears in your desired position.

- Modify group order – expand the tab to the display groups via the Expand button. Next, click the name of the group that you want to reposition and click Move Up or Move down until it appears in the desired position on the list.

- Remove a group from a tab –select the name in the expand Main Tabs list and click Remove command button.

Using Office Add-ins

Excel 2019 supports Office Add-ins to help build your worksheets. These are small app programs that run within specific Office 2019 applications, including Excel, and increase certain functions and boost productivity.

To use Office Add-ins, you have to install them via the following steps:

1. Click the My Add-ins option found in the Insert tab of the Ribbon, then select See All option on the drop-down menu.

2. Click the Store button in the Office Add-ins dialog box to connect to the Office Store.

3. Click desired Office Add-in to purchase (some add-ins are free) then install.

Using Excel's own add-ins

Aside from Office Add-ins, you may also use Excel's own extended features. There are two types of Excel Add-in programs that you can use on Excel 2019:

- Excel Add-ins – this group of add-ins extend data analysis such as Analysis ToolPak, EuroCurrency Tools, and Solver

- Com Add-ins – COM (Component Object Model) add-ins help extend Excel's capability to analyze large amounts of data in data models, such as Inquire, Microsoft Office PowerPivot for Excel, and Power View.

To load these add-ins, you follow these steps:

1. Go to the File menu and click Excel options, then go to the Add-Ins tab.

2. In the Manage drop-down list box, you will see that Excel Add-Ins are selected by default, so to activate COM add-ins, click COM Add-Ins from the Manage dropdown list.

3. Click Go.

PART 2:

The Worksheet Structure

Chapter 3

Facing Your Worksheet

What to expect from this chapter?

- Spreadsheet Design
- Kinds of Cell Entries
- Data Entry, Managing Data, and Saving and Recovery

Spreadsheet Design

Before you start building a spreadsheet in Excel 2019, you should first have a design to follow. The design aspect is usually the easiest in Excel because you can find and borrow designs from other workbooks on the program, aptly called templates.

This chapter teaches you also how to create your own spreadsheet and workbook design from scratch, in case the available templates are not into your liking.

When you open Excel, the Excel Start screen shows you options, such as Opening a new workbook or the Blank Workbook template. If you choose to open a new workbook based on an existing template design, you can do so by clicking the template thumbnail itself. Meanwhile, if you choose the Blank Workbook template, you can immediately begin laying out your new spreadsheet.

Why choose a template

Spreadsheet templates are easier to manage, especially when you already have a projected report in mind. These include budgets, schedules, calendars, as well as invoice and profit and loss statements, among others.

You may also search for other templates based on common searches, such as Business, Personal, Lists, Industry, Calculator, Small Business, Charts, and Finance Management. You may also click the Search for Online Templates text box and type in the keywords describing the template that you want, then click Start Searching.

Do note that aside from using pre-made templates, you can also create your own templates from Excel workbooks.

Once you save a copy of a workbook under a template file, Excel will generate a copy of the said workbook for you to use as a template later on. This way, you can customize the contents of the workbook without modifying the original template.

Saving your customized template

You can save your personalized templates to make the workbooks you create easier to use and quicker to fill up with data. You can do this by making your own labels, slogans, and contact information at the top section of the template.

To save your changes on a template to create a new template file:

1. Click the Save button at the Quick Access toolbar or click File ⇒ Save at the File menu button. You may also click Ctrl+S.

2. Choose the drive and folder where you want to store your personal template files.

3. Click the Save as Type dropdown button then click the Excel template from the list. You may choose to save the template as *.xltx or *xlt if you also intend to use this in earlier versions of Excel (versions 97-2003). If your template contains macros, then you can save it as an Excel Macro-Enabled Template or *.xltm.

4. Click the File Name text box then change the default filename as needed, then click Save to close the Save As dialog box.

5. Click File ⇒ Close or press Alt+FC or Ctrl+W to change the template file.

If you have saved your new template file in another folder, then you need to tell Excel about this too, by following these steps:

1. Click File ⇒Options ⇒ Save or Alt+FTS to open the Excel Options dialog box and choose the Save tab.

2. Click the default Personal Templates Location text box and indicate the complete filename path for the folder where you saved the worksheet template.

3. Click OK to close.

Creating your own template

Aside from modifying already existing templates, you may also create your own spreadsheet template. Many times you may not even be able to do this because while other people generate the type of spreadsheet that you use, their designs are not akin to your needs especially in terms of incorporating and representing the data in a manner that you want.

If you cannot find a pre-made template that fits your needs, then you may go ahead and create your own template. The best way to make your own template is to create an actual workbook prototype, which includes the text, data, formulas, graphics, and macros that you are going to use for it to function.

When preparing a prototype workbook, it is important that you remove all headings, unnecessary text, and numbers that are specific to the prototype and not generic to be included in a template. You may also want to protect the generic data, such as the formulas that compute the values that you and your intended users input on the worksheets created from the template, as well as headings that do not require editing.

Once the layout and content of the prototype are complete, then save the workbook in the template file format so you can generate new workbooks from it.

Meanwhile you may also concert a sample workbook into a template, just follow the steps above but make sure to remove specific data first. You may likewise add comments to certain parts of the template to instruct other users on how to fill these up properly. These comments help when your co-workers are not that familiar with the template or are not that skilled in using Excel.

Opening new workbooks

While you can open a new workbook from the Backstage view of the Excel screen, there are many occasions when you need to open a blank workbook from within the worksheet area, such as when you need to move to a new worksheet while working on an existing workbook.

The best way you can open a blank workbook is to press Ctrl+N. Excel will act by opening a new workbook that carries a generic Book name with the next unused number (Book2, if you started with a workbook named Book1). You can also do the same process in Backstage view by clicking File ⇒ New and then clicking the Blank Workbook thumbnail.

Once you open a blank workbook, Excel makes this document active. To return to the previous workbook, click its button on the Windows taskbar or press Alt+Tab.

Kinds of Cell Entries

When starting to make use of your workbook, you should also know the different types of cell entries. In Excel, all that you enter in any sheet cell is either text or a number.

It is important that you know the type of data you are entering because Excel treats your entry differently, depending on the data it thinks you entered.

Text entries are left-aligned in their cells, and if they consist of more characters than the column's width, the extra characters go over the blank cells in the right column.

Numbers meanwhile are right-aligned in their cells, so if they consist of more characters that the column width, Excel displays a string of number signs across the cell (####).

Labels

When filling in data, all data entries beginning with a letter or punctuation mark are seen as text. A mix of letters and numbers are text, even when the entry starts with a number. All numeric data that contain punctuation other than commas, periods, and forward slashes are also considered text.

Meanwhile, if you begin an entry with an equal sign or the at symbol followed by other characters that are not part of any formula, Excel shows an error when you try to complete the data, as it uses the equal sign to indicate a formula, and that you have not entered a valid formula.

Values

Traditionally, spreadsheets were created to keep financial records, which included a lot of extended totals, subtotals, averages, and grand totals. All these are numbers, and in Excel, number entries are divided into three different categories:

- Numbers that you directly enter in a cell.

- Date and time numbers.

- Numbers computed by formulas.

Numbers that you input into the cells of a worksheet don't change until you specifically change them, by editing or replacing them with new values. When entering numbers, you can mix 0-9 with the following characters:

- + to explicitly say that the number is positive

- () to indicate the number is negative

- $ to indicate currency

- (.) to indicate the decimal point

- Commas (,) between digits to indicate the position of place value,

- % to indicate percentage

For dates, Excel supports two systems, the 1900 system used by Windows and Lotus 123, and the 1904 system used by Macintosh. Dates are stored as special values, and you can tinker with them by going to the Advanced tab of the Excel Options dialog box.

Times of the day are stored as decimal numbers and represent the fraction of a 24-hour period. Excel thus enables you to make time calculations between any two times of the day to determine elapsed time.

Numeric formulas

Numeric entries in a spreadsheet are not usually input directly but are reverted as a calculation by a formula. The numeric formulas you build can do anything from simple calculations to complex statistical analyses.

Since most spreadsheet formulas use numbers that are placed into other cells of the worksheet, and refer to the address of the cell, Excel is able to recalculate the formula and come up with a new result anytime you change values in the original cell.

Basics of Data Entry

Any entry that you make in any cells (empty or otherwise) must be completed with an action, such as hitting Enter or clicking a new cell before it officially becomes the entry of that cell.

Data entry using the keyboard

The only way to entering data from the keyboard is to know the most efficient way to complete the entry in your current cell. You can complete any data entry by pressing the Enter button on the screen, but of course there are certain drawbacks.

When you hit the Enter key, however, Excel automatically completes your entry and moves the cursor to the cell in the next row. But this only works when you are doing a simple entry; you are actually better off when you press the right cursor or the Tab key to complete each entry.

Data entry using the Touch Keyboard

If you are using Excel 2019 on a touchscreen device, you need to open the Windows 10 Touch keyboard in order to enter spreadsheet data.

Constraining data entry to a specific cell range

One of the best ways to enter data into a new table is to preselect the empty cells where the entries should be made then enter the data in this chosen range. But since this trick only works when you know in advance how many columns and rows the new table needs. Thus, preselecting cells helps as it constrains the cell cursor only to that specific range, so long as you press only the keystrokes intended for that action.

The AutoFill feature

Excel has an AutoFill feature that allows you to fill out a series of entries in a data list by entering only the first item in the series. You can use this feature to input row and column headings for a new data table, or to number the records in a data list.

You can also use this feature on a touchscreen device by:

1. Tapping the cell that contains the initial value in the series of that you want AutoFill to extend.

2. Tap and hold the cell until a mini-toolbar appears.

3. Tap the AutoFill button.

4. Drag the AutoFill button through the blank cells in the column or row that the data series sequence should be filled.

Data Validation

The Data Validation feature can be a timesaver when you are doing repetitive data entry, and as well prevent incorrect entries in your sheets. When you use this feature, you can indicate the type of data entry to be done in the cell.

Through Data Validation, you can restrict data entry to a number, specify permissible values for that number, or specify an input message that states an error when you input the wrong entry or a number outside the indicated permissible range.

To use this feature, put the cell cursor in the cell where you want data entry to be restricted and click Data Validation on the Data tab of the Ribbon. A dialog box opens with the Settings tab and see the Allow drop-down list box and select among the following items:

- Any value

- Whole number

- Decimal

- List

- Date

- Time

- Text length

- Custom

Saving your Data

Once you are down with your entries, it is time to save your work. In Excel 2019, you can do this through any of the following steps:

- Click the Save button at the Quick Access toolbar

- Press Ctrl+S or F12

- Click File – Save

Commonly used file formats

When you click the Save As Type drop-down menu, Excel displays a list of file formats that you can use to save the workbook file. These include:

- *.xlsx

- *.xlsm

- *.xls

- *.csv

- *.xml

- *.mhtm or *.mhtml

- *.html

- *.xltx

- *.pdf

- *.xps

- *.odf

Document Recovery

Excel 2019 has a document recovery feature that allows you to keep your files in the event of a computer crash or operating system shutdown. This feature saves your workbooks at regular intervals, and it shows available versions of the workbooks that were open during the time of the crash. It also identifies the original version of the file and when it was saved, together with a recovered version of the same file.

To open a recovered version of a workbook, position the mouse pointer at the AutoRecover version and click its drop-down menu. Then click Open to view the recovered versions so you can choose which version to save.

Chapter 4

Worksheet Formatting

What to expect from this chapter?

- Cell Selections
- Handling Columns and Rows
- Formatting Tables
- Formatting Cells
- Cell Styles
- Conditional Formatting

Formatting is the process where you determine the final look of the worksheet and the data it has. Excel has formatting features that give you great control over the way data appears in your worksheet. For all cell entries, you can assign a font, font size, font style, and color. You can also change the alignment of the entries in a variety of ways-horizontal or vertical, or wrap text entries across the selection.

You may also assign built-in formats for numerical values, and apply different borders or the cells that hold your entries, and place grids on the worksheet itself.

You can format cells and tables on the Quick Analysis tool and the mini-bar that is commonly used for formatting. If the features in this tool is not enough, you may then go to the Table Styles and Cell Styles galleries and the command buttons in the Font, Alignment, and Number groups at the home Tab.

Selecting cells

Selecting cells is often something you have to do when working on Excel. In Excel, you may choose a single cell, a cell range, or discontinuous cell ranges, aka nonadjacent selections.

You can select cells using the mouse, by first going to the cell at the corner of the range. This becomes your first active cell, and after it is the cell range in case you are selecting multiple cells within its range. Once you select your cell(s), drag the pointer to extend the selection until you have highlighted the cells you want to include.

You may also select cells by touch when you are using a tablet or smartphone. You can do this by tapping the first cell in the selection with your finger, and selection handles appear in the upper-left and lower-right corner of the selected cell. Drag or swipe any of the selection handles throughout the rest of the adjacent cells to extend your selection, then choose the entire range.

Lastly, you may also select cells using the keyboard. To use this method, you move the cell cursor to the active cell of the range, then press F8 to see Extend Selection mode, and use the direction keys to move the pointer to the last intended cell range. Excel then chooses all the cells that the cursor covers until you turn off the Extend Selection mode by pressing F8 again. Alternatively, you may use the Shift+click method, by first moving the pointer to the active cell in the range, pressing down the Shift key, then using the direction keys to choose the range. Once you have highlighted the cells you want to include, then release the Shift key.

Handling Columns and Rows

You may also have to adjust columns and rows every once in a while, as this is part of your formatting task on Excel. Column and row sizes also matter especially when you wish to see cell contents in full on your spreadsheet.

Among the formatting tasks for columns and rows on Excel include:

- AutoFit columns and contents – you can do this by positioning the mouse pointer to the right edge of your chosen column and in the column header, and then double click the mouse or double tap your finger or stylus.

- Adjusting the old-fashioned way – meanwhile, if you are not comfortable with AutoFit, you can manually adjust your columns by dragging the mouse pointer to the edge of the chosen column onto the Column header. A

ScreenTip appears above the mouse pointer telling you about formatting options, and you may choose your formatting preferences. Once you have chosen your desired formats, release the mouse button.

- Hiding columns – you can use the Hide command to temporarily secure columns of data from the worksheet. To do this, put the pointer in a chosen cell in that column, click Format and then click Hide & Unhide – Hide Columns from the menu or press Alt+HOUC.

Formatting Tables

Excel 2019 has a Format as Table feature that allows you to format an entire range of data in one operation. You can do this by clicking a new style thumbnail that's found in the Table Styles gallery.

The Table Style Options group has the following boxes that you may check when formatting tables:

- Header Row

- Total Row

- Banded Rows

- First Column

- Last Column

- Banded Columns

You may use the Quick Analysis Tool to format tables. Just select the cells in the table, including the first row and column headings, then the tool will appear on the lower right corner of the cell selection. The Quick Analysis Tool options will then appear, then click the Tables tab to display your formatting options.

Cell Styles

Cell styles make use of different formatting aspects such as number format, text alignment, fonts and font sizes, borders, fills, and protection options. They can be found in the Cell Styles gallery at the Cell Styles button on the Ribbon's Home tab.

Creating a new cell style

You may also create a new cell style by means of the following steps:

1. Place the cell pointer in a cell that has no Excel default formatting applied to it, then click New Cell Style.

2. Type a name for the style that you are creating in the Style Name text box.

3. Uncheck the check boxes of any attributes you don't wish to include in your newly created style.

4. Click the Format button located below the Style Name text box to access other cell formatting options.

5. Once you finish dedicating formatting attributes, click OK and return to the Style dialog box.

6. Click OK to close.

Conditional Formatting

In Excel 2019, you have the option Conditional Formatting that allows you to format a range of values so that unwanted or unusual values, such as those outside certain limits, are automatically formatted. You can find the Conditional Formatting button in the Styles thumbnail on the Home tab, and comes with a drop-down menu with the following options:

- Highlight Cells Rules – contains various options for defining formatting rules for cells that have certain values, dates, or text that fall within a particular range of values.

- Top/Bottom Rules – a menu with different options for defining formatting rules for top and bottom values, average values, percentages, etc.

- Data bars – is a palette of different color data bars that can be used to indicate the values of a cell selection.

- Color Scales – palette with different colored scales that can be used to indicate values of a cell selection by clicking the color scale thumbnail.

- Icon Sets – palette of different icons that can be applied to the cell selection to indicate various conditions applied to a various threshold values.

- New Rule – define a custom conditional formatting rule to apply on the cell selection.

- Clear Rules – a continuation menu where you can remove conditional formatting rules for your cell selection.

- Manage Rules – takes you to the Conditional Formatting Rules Manager where you can edit particular rules and adjust rule precedence.

Chapter 5

Printing Your Worksheet

What to expect from this chapter?

- Different ways to Print
- Page Setup Options
- Using Print Options
- Headers and Footers
- Page Break Issues and How to Solve Them
- Printing Formulas

There are a lot of instances when you are tasked to print your spreadsheets, and this can be really tricky. The good thing is, Excel makes it easy to print out professional-looking reports from your spreadsheet data.

This chapter focuses on the different printing techniques that you can do in Excel, including tweaks to customize printouts according to your preferences.

Different ways to print

Printing from Backstage View

One of the easiest ways to print your spreadsheet is through the Excel 2019 Backstage view, which contains a Print screen which you can open by clicking File – Print, or press Ctrl+P. Through this method, you can:

- Change the number of spreadsheet copies to be printed

- Click the name of the printer to use when printing the spreadsheet

- Choose the part of the spreadsheet to be printed – between Print Active Sheets, Print Entire Workbook, or Print Selection

- Print both sides of the paper through the Print on Both Sides, Flip Pages on Long Edge, or Print on Both Sides, Flip Pages on Short Edge options

- Print multiple copies of the spreadsheet

- Change the paper orientation from portrait to landscape

- Change paper size

- Change margins

Quick Printing

If you are comfortable with the default print settings on Excel, then you can easily print your worksheets. Just add the Quick Print button to the Quick Access Toolbar by clicking the Customize Quick Access and choose the Quick Print item from the menu.

Once you have added the Quick Print button, you can use it to print a copy of the entire contents of the current worksheet. Excel routes the print job to the print queue, then sends the job to the printer to proceed with the appropriate action.

To stop the printing, click Cancel in the Print dialog box.

Page Setup Options

One thing that's tricky about printing a spreadsheet is that it can be complex to figure out how to get the pages right. This can be addressed however, by the getting to know the options at the Page Setup group found at the Ribbon's Page Layout tab.

There are two groups at the Page Layout Tab that you can use when formatting your worksheet pages: the Page Setup and the Scale to Fit.

The Page Setup Controls

You may tinker with Page Setup controls by getting to know the following commands:

- Margins – you may choose one of three preset margins or set custom margins on the Margins tab

- Orientation –choose between Portrait and Landscape mode

- Size – select a preset paper size or set a custom size to change printing resolution or page number

- Print Area – clear the Print area

- Breaks – insert or delete page breaks

- Background – you may choose a graphic image to be used as a background for all worksheets in your workbook

- Print Titles – via the Sheet tab of the Page Setup, you can define rows of the worksheet to repeat with the top columns to serve as print titles for the report.

Scale to Fit Controls

You may use this if your printer supports scaling options. You can get a worksheet to fit on a single page by choosing the 1 Page option on the Width and Height menu attached to the command button. When you choose these options, Excel finds a way to reduce the size of the information that you intend to print and fit it all on a single page.

Using Print Options

The Print section of the Page Setup box (Alt+PSP) has useful options and a couple of drop-down options that you should be aware of. These include:

- Gridlines

- Comments

- Cell errors

- Black and White

- Draft Quality

- Row and Column Headings

None of these options are preselected, so you can tinker with them in case you want to make changes on the quality of your worksheet printout.

Headers and Footers

Headers and footers are standard text that appears on each page of a spreadsheet report. A header is found on top of the page, while the footer is at the bottom margin. Excel does not automatically add a header or footer on a new workbook, unless you specify it.

These are used to identify the document used to produce a report and display page numbers as well as the time and date of printing.

You can add a header or footer at the Page Layout view by clicking Page Layout View on the Status bar. Once the worksheet is displayed in this view, point the mouse over the section in the top margin of the first page marked "Add Header", or at the bottom of the first page marked "Add Footer."

Page Break Issues and How to Solve Them

Excel has a Page Break Preview feature that allows you to spot page break issues and fix them right away. You can rectify such problems by means of the following steps:

1. Click the Page Break Preview button on the Status bar or Alt+WI

2. Position the mouse pointer on the page break indicator

3. After adjusting the page breaks, click the Normal button

You may also insert page breaks manually at the cell cursor's position by selecting Insert Page Break on the Page Layout tab (Alt+PBI) and remove them by choosing Remove Page Break or (Alt+PBR).

Printing Formulas

Apart from printing spreadsheets, you should also learn how to print formulas in a worksheet report. You can go through a printout of formulas in your worksheet to ensure that you haven't made any mistake before you distribute your report to targeted recipients.

To do this, you have to first display the formulas in the cells by clicking Show Formulas in Formula Auditing group (fx) or Alt+MH.

Excel displays the contents of each cell as they appear on the Formula bar. It allows you to go between the normal cell display and formula cell display by pressing Ctrl+`.

Once Excel displays the formulas, you may then proceed with printing as you would on a regular spreadsheet report.

PART 3:

Functions, Formulas and How to Use Them

Chapter 6

Basic Formulas

What to expect from this chapter?

- Formulas You Need to Know
- How to Copy Formulas
- Adding Array Formulas
- Range Names
- Linking Formulas
- Formula Recalculation
- Circular References

Formulas are the life of the worksheet. Without them, the spreadsheet would be no better than its paper equivalent. The good thing is, in Excel provides you the ability to do your computations right on the cells of the worksheet without using a separate calculator.

The formulas that you build and use can be simple to complex, but they rely heavily on the use of operators or built-in functions, which both describe the computation to perform and the order on how to perform it.

When you use functions on your formulas, you need to learn the kind of information that function uses, known as argument(s).

What you need to know about formulas

Formulas vary from simple addition to complex ANOVA statistical variation, but they all have one thing in common: they all begin with the equal sign (=).

When creating a formula that uses a built-in function, you usually use the Insert Function on the formula bar to choose and insert the said function. Excel responds by adding the opening equal sign.

Building formulas

You can build formulas manually by typing in the cell addresses or pointing to them in the worksheet. Using the Pointing technique is easier when building original formulas to avoid creating mistakes when typing cell addresses.

When using the Pointing method, you stop and click the cell or drag over the cell range after typing the operator in the formula. Meanwhile, when using the same method to build a formula under a built-in function, click the cell or drag through the cell range to be used in defining the function's arguments in the Function Arguments dialog box.

Using the Insert Function

Excel has a variety of built-in functions that you can use when building formulas. To use them, you may start by going to the Insert Function button on the Formula bar (fx) to display the dialog box. You can then choose its options and find the function that you want to use and define the argument that the function needs to perform a calculation.

How to Copy Formulas

Copying formulas are among the easiest tasks to do in a spreadsheet activity that relies on formulas. When a formula uses cell references, Excel copies an original formula to every place that requires a similar location.

Excel does this by automatically adjusting the cell references from the original formula in order to fit the position of the copies you intend to make, via a system called *relative cell addresses.*

Array Formulas

A lot of spreadsheet tables use an original formula that is copied to adjacent cells. However, there are cases when you can create the original formula so that Excel does the calculation not just on the active cell, but also on all other cells where you would copy the formula.

You can do this by creating an *array formula,* which a special formula that operates under a range of values. if a   cell range supplies this range, it is called "array range." If this range is supplied by numerical values, they are referred to as an "array constant."

Editing an array formula is slightly different, as you must treat the range as a single unit and revise it in only one operation. This means that you cannot move, edit, clear, insert or delete individual cells in the range.

To do the edits, choose a cell in the array range than active Edit mode by clicking the formula or going to the Formula bar (F2). Excel then shows the contents of the array formula and outlines the ranges referred to the array formula in the cells in different colors that correspond to those assigned to the range addresses in the edited formula.

Once you make your changes, press Ctrl+Shift+Enter to enter these edits and make Excel enclose the array formula in a brace.

Range Names

While cell references offer a convenient means to point out a cell location in the worksheet, they are not descriptive of their function when used in formulas. Luckily, Excel has a way to make it easier to assign descriptive names to the cells, cell ranges, constants, and as well as the formulas that make their function on the worksheet look more understandable.

When you assign a name to a certain cell range, you can locate and choose all the cells in that range using the Go To dialog box. Click Go To from the Find and Select button's drop-down menu on the Home tab (Ctrl+G or F5). Excel then chooses the entire range and shifts the worksheet display so that you can view the first cell in that range.

Linking Formulas

Linking formulas are formulas that move or transfer a constant or another formula to a new place in the worksheet, workbook, or a different workbook without copying it to its new location.

When you build a linking formula, it uses the constant formula to a new location so that the result in the linking formula stays tied to the original. If you edit the original constant or any of the cells sourced to in the original formula, the result in the cell holding the linked formula is updated at the same time as well.

You can create a linking formula using two ways:

1. Select the cell where you want to place the linking formula by typing =, and then click the cell with the constant or the formula that you want to bring to that cell. Then complete the entry by pressing Enter.

2. Select the cell with the formula or constant that you want to bring to a new location then hit the Copy button or

Ctrl+C. Then click the cell where the linking formula is to be set before you choose the Paste Link option.

When you use the first method, Excel uses a relative cell reference to refer to the cell that has the formula. However, if you use the second method, Excel uses an absolute cell reference to refer to the original cell.

When you make a linking formula to a cell on a different sheet of the same workbook, Excel will insert the worksheet name in front of the cell address. When you make a linking formula to a cell in another workbook, Excel inserts the workbook name enclosed in square brackets before the worksheet name.

Formula Recalculation

Excel usually recalculates worksheets automatically as soon as you change formulas, entries, or names on which the formulas rely on. This system works without errors so long as the worksheet is not too big or does not contain tables with complex values.

When Excel calculates your worksheet, it recalculates only the cells affected by the changes that you have made. Meanwhile, in a complex worksheet with a wide array of formulas, recalculation may take more time.

To control when Excel makes its calculation on your worksheet, click the Calculation Options on the Formulas tab, then go to

Manual option or Alt+MXM. This allows Excel to display a message "Calculate" on the Status bar, and it calculates only when you hit Calculate Now (F9).

Circular References

A circular reference is one that depends on its own value. This usually occurs when you refer in the formula to the cell you are building the formula itself.

Let's say that cell B10 is active when you build this formula: =A10+B10

When you click the Enter button to insert this formula in B10, Excel shows an Alert dialog box saying that it cannot calculate the formula due to the circular reference. You can press Enter to close the Alert, and Excel shows the general information about circular references.

Some circular references can be solved by increasing the number of times they are to be recalculated, while others need to be removed from the spreadsheet.

Chapter 7

Error Trapping and Logical Functions

What to expect from this chapter?

- Error Values
- Error Trapping Formulas
- Logical Functions
- Formula Auditing
- Removing Errors

Identifying and rectifying formula errors is also vital in Excel. In this chapter, you see how to locate the source of formula errors so that you can fix them right away.

Perhaps the most annoying problem with errors, aside from the #REF! and #DIV/0! is that they tend to spread across the workbook to other cells that have the formulas that are linked to their erroneous cells.

If you are working on a large worksheet, you may not be able to tell which cell contains the formula error. To fix this, you have to learn the technique called "error trapping."

Error Values

There are times when Excel cannot properly calculate a formula that you enter, so it shows an error value. It uses various error values that begin with the number sign (#).

If a formula contains a reference to a cell that brings back an error, it returns that error value as well. This may cause error values to be displayed on the worksheet, making it hard for you to tell which cell contains the formula that caused the source error and fix the problem.

Error Trapping

There are instances when you already know ahead of time that some error values are inevitable in a worksheet as long as they are missing some data, which will display #DIV/0!

Some people choose to remove the display of zero values from a template that contains error-trapping formulas to that no one is able to interpret the zeros as the correct value for the said formula.

To remove the display of zeros from a worksheet, go to the Excel Options and head to the Advanced section. Uncheck the Show a Zero in Cells that Have Zero Values check box in the Display Options area, or File – Options or Alt+FT. with this action, the cells with error-trapping formulas stay blank until you provide them with data needed to produce the right answers.

Logical Functions

To identify errors, Excel uses logical functions that appear on the Logical command button on the Formulas tab of the Ribbon (Alt+ML). Logical functions display either TRUE or FALSE to the cells where the functions are evaluated. Among the functions along with their corresponding argument syntax are:

- IF(*logical_exp,value_if_true,value_if_false*) — evaluates whether the *logical_exp* expression is TRUE or FALSE. If TRUE, the IF function uses the *value_if_true* argument and returns it to the cell. If FALSE, the IF function uses the *value_if_false* argument and returns it to the cell.

- IFERROR(*value,value_if_error*) — returns the *value* argument when the cell referred to in another logical argument in which the IFERROR function is used doesn't contain an error value and the *value_if_error* argument when it does.

- IFNA(*value,value_if_na*) — returns the *value* argument when the cell referred to in another logical argument in which the IFNA function is used doesn't contain #NA and the *value_if_error* argument when it does.

- IFS(*logical_test1,value_if_true1*) — evaluates whether or not one or more *logical_test* arguments are TRUE.

- AND(*logical_exp1,logical_exp2,...*) — evaluates whether the *logical_exp* arguments are TRUE or FALSE. If all expressions are TRUE, the AND function returns TRUE to the cell. If any of them are FALSE, the AND function returns FALSE.

- OR(*logical_exp1,logical_exp2,...*) — evaluates whether the *logical_exp* arguments are TRUE or FALSE. If any expressions are TRUE, the OR function returns TRUE. If all are FALSE, the OR function returns FALSE.

- XOR(*logical_exp1,logical_exp2,...*) — evaluates whether the *logical_exp* arguments (usually in an array) are predominantly TRUE or FALSE. When the number of TRUE inputs is odd, the XOR function returns TRUE. When the number of TRUE inputs is even, the XOR function returns FALSE.

- SWITCH(*expression,value1,result1,[default]*) — tests the value returned by the *expression* argument against a list of value arguments (*value1*, *value2*, and so on to *value126*) and returns the corresponding result (*result1* for *value1*, *result2* for *value2*, and so on to *result126* for *value126*) when a match is TRUE. Optional *default* argument is returned when none of the value arguments match the expression argument. When no *default* argument is specified, Excel returns the #NA error value when there is no match.

- TRUE( ) — returns TRUE in its cell without condition.

- FALSE( ) — returns FALSE in its cell without condition.

The logical_test and logical arguments for these logical functions normally use the comparison operators (=, <, >, <=, >=, or <>), which result to logical TRUE or logical FALSE values.

Formula Auditing

If you don't get to trap error values before they get into the spreadsheet, you will have to track down the original cell that caused all the issues and fix it. Excel has some effective formula-auditing tolls that can be used to track down the cell that causes the problem by tracing the relationships between the formulas found on your worksheet.

You can then see which cells, referred to as *direct precedents*, directly feed formulas and which cells, called dependents, rely on the results of the formulas. The program even has a way to backtrack the potential sources of error values of a particular cell.

The formula-auditing tools are located in the command buttons at the Formula Auditing group on the Formulas Tab. These include:

- Trace Precedents – when you click this button, Excel points arrows to the cells (direct precedents) inside the chosen cell. Clicking it a second time adds tracer arrows that display the cells (indirect precedents) that are referred in the formulas in the direct precedents.

- Trace Dependents – Excel draws arrows from the chosen cell to the direct dependents. Clicking it a second time adds tracer arrows to identify the indirect dependents that link to the formulas found in the direct dependents.

- Remove Arrows – removes all the drawn arrows.

- Show Formulas – display all the formulas in their cells in the worksheet rather than their calculated values.

- Error Checking – clicking this button displays the Error checking dialog box, which describes the error in the current cell and helps you trace its precedents.

- Evaluate Formula – opens the Evaluate Formula dialog box, where you can make Excel evaluate all parts of the formula in the current cell.

- Watch Window – opens the Watch Window dialog box which shows the workbook, sheet, cell location, range name, current value, and formula in cells that you add to the watch list. To add a cell, click the cell in the worksheet, click Add Watch button, then click Add in the Add Watch dialog box.

Error Checking

When a formula produces an error value aside from #N/A in a cell, Excel displays a tiny error indicator in the upper left corner of the cell. An alert options button appears to that part of the cell whenever you make it active.

When you click the drop-down button to check errors, a menu appears, showing an item with the name of the error value followed by the following:

- Help on this Error

- Show Calculation Steps

- Ignore Error

- Edit in Formula Bar

- Error Checking Options

Removing Errors in Printout

There are instances when you don't have the time to catch all the potential formula errors or track them down and get rid of them before you print out and distribute the spreadsheet. In this case, you may have to remove the display of all the error values before you actually print the report.

You can do this by clicking the Sheet tab on the Page Setup. Click the Sheet tab in the Page Setup and then click the drop-down menu attached to Cell Errors As dropdown List box.

The default value for this list is Displayed, so you have all errors displayed on the printout exactly as they are shown on the worksheet. This list also has the following items that you can click to remove the display of error values:

- Click the <blank> option to replace all error values with blank cells.

- Click the - - option to replace all error values with two dashes.

- Click the #N/A option to replace all error values (except for #N/A

- entries, of course) with the special #N/A value (which is considered an

- error value when you select the <blank> or — options).

Chapter 8

Date and Time

What to expect from this chapter?

- Understanding Date and Time
- Date Functions
- Time Functions

Understanding Date and Time

In Excel, dates and times are not treated as text entries. Any entry with a format that looks like one of the date and time number formats being used by the program is converted into a serial number. For dates, this serial number shows the number of days that have gone by since the start of the 20th century so that January 1, 1900 uses a serial number of 1, January 2, 1900 uses a serial number of 2, and so on.

For times, this serial number is a fraction that represents the number of hours, minutes and seconds that have gone since midnight. This begins with serial number 0.00000000, so that

12:00:00 pm is serial number 0.50000000, while 10:00:00 pm is 0.9166666667, and on.

As long as you set a numeric entry that adheres to a recognized date or time format, Excel sees it as a date or time serial number. Only when you input a formatted date or time as a text entry, or import times and dates as text entries into the worksheet, should you worry about converting them into time and date serial numbers for Excel to make calculations on them.

Formulas that calculate elapsed dates

Most date formulas are designed to compute the number of days or years that have elapsed between two dates. To do this, you have to build a simple formula that subtracts the earlier date from the later date.

Formulas that calculate elapsed times

There are spreadsheets that require that formulas calculate the amount of elapsed time between a starting and ending time. To build a formula that computes how much time has elapsed, subtract the starting time of the day from the ending time of the day.

Date functions

Excel has a number of built-in Date functions that you may use on your spreadsheet. You may even find more of these functions when you install the an add-in. Among the most common functions for date are:

- TODAY – this function has no arguments and is always entered as "=TODAY()". When you enter this function in a cell, Excel returns the current date using the following format: 5/13/2019.

- DATE and DATEVALUE – the DATE function returns a date serial number for the date specified by year, month, and day. This function has the following syntax: (DATE(year,month,day). This function helps when you have a worksheet that has different parts of the date in separate columns. You can use this function to combine three columns of date information into a single date cell.

- DAY, WEEKDAY, MONTH, AND YEAR – these functions all show just parts of the date serial number that you specify as their argument.

  - DAY(*serial_num*) to return the day of the month in the date (as a number between 1 and 31).

  - WEEKDAY(*serial_num*,[*return_type*]) to return the day of the week (as a number from 1 to 7 or 0 to 6). The optional *return_type* argument is a number between 1 and 3; 1 (or no *return_type* argument) designates the first type where 1 means Sunday and 7 means Saturday; 2 designates the second type where 1 means Monday and 7 means Sunday; and 3 designates the third type where 0 means Monday and 6 means Sunday.

- o MONTH(*serial_num*) to return the number of the month in the date serial number (from 1 to 12).

- o YEAR(*serial_num*) to return the number of the year (as an integer between 1900 and 9999) in the date serial number.

- DAYS360 – this function returns the number of days between two dates that's based on a 360-day year.

- EDATE – (elapsed date) this function computes a past date or future date that is lots of months ahead or behind the date that you designate as its start_date argument.

- EOMONTH – (end of month) this function computes the last day of the month that is either so many months ahead or behind the date that you state as your start_date argument.

- NETWORKDAYS – this function returns the number of work days that are present in a starting and ending date that you designate as arguments.

- WEEKNUM – this function shows a number indicating where the week in a particular date falls within a year.

- WORKDAY – this function is used to find out the date that is so many workdays either before or after a certain date.

- YEARFRAC – this function allows you to calculate the fraction of the year which is computed from the number of days between dates.

Time Functions

Excel offers few Time functions, but like Date functions, the Time functions allow you to convert text entries that represent times of day into time serial numbers so that they can be used in calculations.

The Time functions also include functions for merging parts of a time into a single serial number, and extracting the hours, minutes, and seconds from a single time serial number. Such functions include:

- NOW – this function gives you current time and date based on your device's internal clock.

- TIME AND TIMEVALUE – this function allows you to create a decimal number that represents a time serial number, ranging from 0 to 0.99999999, and representing time 0:00:00 to 23:59:59.

- HOUR, MINUTE, and SECOND – these functions allow you to extract parts of a time value in the spreadsheet.

Chapter 9

Financial Formulas

What to expect from this chapter?

- Basics of Financial Functions
- PV, NPV, FV, and PMT
- Depreciation

Spreadsheets were created to keep tabs on financial calculations, thus Excel contains a number of sophisticated financial functions to determine things such as present, future, or net present value of a certain investment. It also has functions that determine payment, number of periods, principal or interest part of a payment on a loan, rate of return on an investment, or the depreciation of assets.

Basics of Financial Functions

To be able to understand and utilize Excel's financial functions, you must first understand the jargon used in their arguments. Most of these are under PV (present value), NPV (net present value), FV (future value), PMT (payment), and IPMT (interest payment).

- **PV** refers to the present value or the principal amount of the annuity.

- **FV** refers to the future value or the principal plus interest on the annuity.

- **PMT** refers to the payment made each period in the annuity.

- **RATE** refers to the interest rate per period.

- **NPER** refers to the sum all of payment periods throughout the life of the annuity.

When using financial functions, remember that the fv, pv, and pmt arguments can be either positive or negative, and they depend on whether you are receiving money or paying out money. Also, you would like to express the rate argument in the same unit as the nper argument, so if you make payments on a loan and you express the nper as the total number of monthly payments, you need to express the interest rate in monthly terms as well.

PV, NPV and FV

You can find the PV, NPV and FV functions by going to the Formulas tab (Alt+MI), clicking on the Financial button and resorting to the drop-down list. These functions enable you to see the profitability of an investment.

Computing for present value

The PV function returns the present value of an investment made, which is the total amount in a series of future payments is worth at present. The syntax for this function is as follows:

=PV(rate,nper,pmt,[fv],[type])

The fv and type arguments in this context are optional. The fv argument is the future value or cash balance that you want to get after completing your last payment. If you remove the fv argument, Excel will assume that a future value of zero. The type argument meanwhile indicates if the payment is made at the beginning or end of the period. Leaving the type argument blank or putting a 0 means the payment is made at the end of the period while using 1 sets the payment at the beginning of the period.

Net present value

The NPV function computes the net present value via a series of cash flows. The syntax for this function is

=NPV(rate,value1,[value2],[value3][...])

Value1, Value2, Value3 and so on are between 1 and 13 value arguments and represent a series of payments (negative values)

and income (positive values). Each of these is spaced in time and occurs at the end of the period.

The NPV investment starts one period before the period of value1 cash flow, the ends with the last cash flow in the series.

Computing for future value

The FV function meanwhile computes for the future value of an investment, with the syntax:

=FV(rate,nper,pmt,[pv],[type])

The rate, nper, pmt, and type arguments are also the same as those used in the PV function.

The pv argument is the present value for which you want to compute the future value. As with the fv and type arguments, both the pv and type arguments are optional.

If you remove these arguments, Excel will think that their values are zero in the function/

You can use this function to compute the future value of an investment, such as an individual retirement account.

PMT Function

The PMT function can be found in the Financial button of the Formulas tab, and it calculates the periodic payment for an annuity, based on the assumption that a stream of equal payments and a constant interest. It used the following syntax:

=PMT(rate,nper,pv,[fv],[type])

Just like other financial functions, rate is the interest rate per period, nper is the number of periods, pv is the present value, fv is the future value or cash balance that you want after completing your last payment, and type is the value 0 for payments done at the end of the period or 1 for payments made at the beginning of the period.

Depreciation Functions

Excel also lets you use four different depreciation functions, with each having a slightly different way of determining depreciation of an asset over time. These depreciation functions are found on the Financial button of the Formulas tab, and include:

- SLN(*cost,salvage,life*) refers to the straight-line calculation method for returning the depreciation of an asset for a single period

- SYD(*cost,salvage,life,per*) refers to the sum-of-years-digits depreciation calculation method

- DB(*cost,salvage,life,period,[month]*) refers to the fixed-declining balance calculation method

- DDB(*cost,salvage,life,period,[factor]*) refers to the double-declining balance calculation method

If you may notice, aside from the optional month argument in the DB function and the optional factor argument in the DDB function, all depreciation functions require arguments such as cost, salvage, and life. All but the SLN function need a period argument too:

- *Cost* is the asset's initial cost that you are depreciating.

- *Salvage* is the asset's value at the end of the depreciation (also

- recognized asset's salvage value).

- *Life* is the number of periods over which the asset is depreciating (also

- recognized as the asset's useful life).

- *Per* or *period* is the period over which the asset is being depreciated.

The units used in the period argument must be the same as those used in the life argument, so if you express the life argument in years, you should also express the period argument in years.

Do note that the DB function may accept the optional month argument. When omitted, Excel assumes that the number of months to be 12.

When using the DDB function to compute double declining balance, you may add an optional factor argument. This is the rate at which the balance declines in the depreciation schedule.

Chapter 10

Math and Statistical Formulas

What to expect from this chapter?

- Math and Trigonometry Functions
- Statistical Functions

In Excel, Math and Trig functions are located at the Math and Trig command button in the Formulas tab. This category covers all specialized trigonometric functions like those that compute for sine, cosine, and tangent of different angles and logarithmic functions, as well as common math functions for summing numbers, rounding up and down, raising numbers to a certain power, and finding the square root.

One of the most recently added functions in Excel 2019 is the Arabic function, which converts any roman numeral text into Arabic numerals (xxi to 21). This function complements the older Roman function, which convers Arabic numerals into Roman numeral text.

Statistical functions meanwhile are found in a continuation menu that can be accessed through the More Functions command at the Formulas tabs. They include common functions such as average, highest and lowest values in a cell range, and as well sophisticated functions that compute chi-squared distribution, binomial distribution, frequency, variance, standard deviation, and skewness of distribution.

Math and Trigonometry Functions

This category can be found at the Math and Trig command button at the Formulas tab (Alt+MG). it groups all specialized trigonometric functions as well as common arithmetic functions.

Under this category are functions such as SUM, INT, EVEN, ODD, ROUND, TRUNC, PRODUCT, SUMPRODUCT, SUMSQ, and SQRT.

Rounding off

The ROUND function is used to round up or down fractional values in a worksheet. This function changes the way Excel stores the number in a cell that contains the said function. It uses the following syntax:

ROUND(number,number_of_digits)

The number argument is the value that you want to round off, and the number_of_digits is the number of digits that you want the number to be rounded.

You may also use the ROUNDUP or ROUNDDOWN function. Both functions take the same number and number_of_digits as the ROUND function; however, the ROUNDUP function rounds up the value specified by the number argument, while the ROUNDDOWN function rounds the value down.

INT and TRUNC

You may also use the INT (integer) and TRUNC (truncate) functions to round off values. These functions are used only when you don't have to think of all or part of the fractional portion of the value.

When you use INT, it only requires a single number argument, and Excel rounds the valued own to its nearest integer, with the syntax =INT(A3).

The TRUNC function meanwhile uses the same number and number_of_digits as the ROUND, ROUNDUP, and ROUNDDOWN, except that the number_of_digits is purely optional. This function doesn't round off the number, but truncates the number to the nearest integer by removing the fractional part of the said number.

Odd and Even

Excel has EVEN and ODD functions that also work to round off numbers. The EVEN function rounds the value as its number argument up to the nearest even integer. Meanwhile, the ODD function rounds the value up to the nearest odd integer.

Ceiling

The CEILING.MATH function allows you to just round up a number, but set the multiple of significance to be used for rounding. This function is useful when working on figures that need rounding to specific units.

The CEILING.MATH function used the syntax:

CEILING.MATH(number,[significance],[mode])

POWER and SQRT

While you can use the caret operator to build a formula that pulls up a number to any power, you also have to be aware that Excel has a math function called POWER, and it accomplishes the same task. You may use the following exponentiation syntax:

=POWER(num, num_digit)

Meanwhile, the SQRT function allows you to calculate the square root of any number. For example, if you use QRT to build this formula in a cell:

=SQRT(81)

Excel gives an answer 9 into that cell.

Do note that the SQRT function cannot work on negative numbers, and if you try to do so, it will show a #NUM! error value. To avoid this, you may use the ABS (absolute) math function, which gives the absolute value of the number (number without a sign).

Statistical Functions

Excel also has the most complete set of statistical functions that are available outside a dedicated statistics software application (such as SPSS). If you want to use these functions from the Formulas tab, click More Functions then highlight the Statistical option at the very top of the menu or press Alt+MQS.

The most common statistical functions are that of AVERAGE, MAX, and MIN, but you may also tinker on the more complex CHITEST, POISSON, and PERCENTILE functions, among others.

Average, MAX, and MIN

These functions are commonly used for statistical tasks as they are useful to number crunchers and dedicated statisticians. These functions follow the same syntax, and use the same arguments.

=AVERAGE(*number1*,[*number2*],[...])

Counting cells

There are also times when you need to know how many cells are there in certain cell range, row, column, or worksheet. There are times when you need to know how many cells are still blank and how many are occupied, how many have text or numerical entries.

Excel has various counting functions that you can use, and these can tell you the type of entry your selected cells contain. You can do so by using the following:

- COUNTA – to count the number of occupied cells

- COUNTIF – the function for conditional counting, such as when cells meet a certain condition

Specialized statistical functions

You may also use built-in stat functions in the Statistical category in the Insert Function dialog box. Excel also has a set of special analysis tools in the AnalysisToolPak – VBA add-ins. These include ANOVA, F-Test, rank and percentile, t-Test, and Fourier Analysis.

PART 4:

Worksheet Collaboration, Review, and Protection

Chapter 11

Protecting Your Workbook and Worksheet Data

What to expect from this chapter?

- Password Protecting the File
- Protecting Your Worksheet

After preparing a worksheet report, you have to send this out for review. However, your worksheet contains delicate data that can be distorted during review when not properly protected, thus you need to make them secure.

In Excel 2019, there are two levels in which you can secure your data. The first is by protecting the workbook file itself so that only chosen users with a password can open it to view, print, or edit the data. The other means of protection is on the worksheets themselves, where only people with the password can make changes to its content and structure.

When it comes to protecting the integrity of the spreadsheet, you can decide which parts of the sheets can users change, and those that they cannot.

Protecting the Workbook with a Password

When you password-protect a workbook, you can prevent other unauthorized users to opening the said file, or editing it. You can set a password for opening the workbook when you are working on a spreadsheet whose data is of sensitive nature and only a certain group of people in your organization should be granted to view, edit, and make other changes to it. Such data include personal information, employee salaries, financial figures, etc.

Once you have set a password to open the workbook, you should supply this password to the people who need access to it.

You also set a password for changing the workbook when you are dealing with a spreadsheet that needs to be viewed and printed by other users, none of who are authorized to make any modifications to the entries. For instance, you may assign a password to modify a workbook for your boss, and another password simply for viewing and printing purposes to a temp or intern.

Protecting the workbook when saving the file itself

If you are working on a particular spreadsheet that contains sensitive data and you want to restrict access to certain folks, consider setting a password for opening it as well as a separate password for specifically modifying the file.

You can do this through the following steps:

1. Go to the File menu and click Save As or use the Alt+FA keyboard sequence within Excel.

2. Double-click Browse to bring up the Save As dialog.

3. Within the dialog, click the Tools drop-down button and choose General Options. This will provide you with a window to enter a password to open and/or a password to modify the File Sharing section.

4. Assign a password in the corresponding fields. Passwords can stretch up to 255 characters consisting of a combination of letters, numbers, and spaces. Do note that passwords are case-sensitive so you can use a combination of upper and lower-case letters. As you key in your password, Excel masks the characters by rendering them as dots.

5. Confirm the passwords you entered earlier just to make sure you didn't make any mistakes in setting them.

6. Click the OK button to close the General Options dialog box.

7. Type the password exactly as you placed it in the Password to Open text box (or Password to Modify text box, if you did not use the Password to Open text box), and then click OK.

8. If you want to save the now protected version of the workbook under another filename or in a different location edit the name in the File Name text box then choose the new location or folder from the Save In drop-down menu.

9. Click the Save button to seal that password into the workbook .

Assigning a password to access the workbook from the Info screen

Another way to assign the password to open your workbook is by doing it on Excel 2019's Info screen, which can be found in the Backstage view. You can do this via the following steps:

1. Click File -> Info or press Alt+FI to open the Info screen.

2. Click the Protect Workbook button to open the drop-down menu and select Encrypt with Password.

3. Type the password the same way as you entered it in the Password text box and then click OK.

4. Key in the password in the Reenter Password text box the same way you entered it into the Password text box in the Encrypt Document dialog box, then hit OK. Do note that when you do not replicate the password, Excel shows an alert dialog box that says that the confirmation password is not identical. Once you click OK to close this alert dialog box, you are taken back to the Confirm Password dialog box. Once you successfully replicate the password, Excel closes the Confirm Password dialog box and takes you back to the Info screen where "A password is required to open this workbook" status appears.

5. Click the Save option found on the Info screen.

Entering the password to access the workbook

Once you save a workbook file to which you've designated a password to access it, you should be able to reproduce the password to open the file. When you try to open the workbook, Excel shows a Password dialog box, where you should enter the password the same way as you assigned it to the file.

If you enter the wrong password, Excel will display an alert box notifying you of the error. When you click OK to close that alert message, you will be taken back to the original Excel window where you have to repeat the entire file-opening process.

Once you supply the right password, Excel opens the workbook for viewing and printing (and editing, unless you have assigned a password to modify the file).

You may also get rid of the password on the file by clicking File -> Save As or pressing Alt+FA, then selecting General Options from the Tools menu. From there, you can delete the password in the Password to Open text dialog then click OK in the General Options dialog box and the Save button in the Save As dialog. By doing this, Excel resaves the workbook file without a password.

Entering the password to make modifications

If you have protected your workbook from changes using the Password to Modify option, Excel displays the Password dialog box where you should accurately reproduce the password assigned for modification or click the Read Only button to open the workbook as a Read Only file.

When you supply the right password, Excel closes the Password dialog box, and you are free to make changes on the workbook in any way you wish.

Changing or removing a password

When changing or deleting a password, you should first supply the current password that you want to change to get the workbook open. All you have to do is change or remove the password in the Info screen at the Backstage view.

Protecting the Worksheet

Once you have your worksheet the way you intend it to be, you will need Excel's Protection feature to keep it that way. There are ways to keep the formulas and text in a spreadsheet protected from unnecessary changes. You can do this by using the Protect Sheet and Protect Workbook command options found at the Review Tab.

All cells in your workbook are locked or unlocked for editing, and hidden or unhidden for viewing. When you start a new spreadsheet, all the cells have locked as their editing status and unhidden as their display status, but this default setting does nothing until you turn on the protection using the Protect Sheet and Protect Workbook commands.

When building your spreadsheet templates, you would want to unlock all the cells where users need to enter data and keep locked the cells that contain headings and formulas that should never be changed. You may also want to hide the cells with formulas if you are concerned that their display might tempt users to tinker with them.

You can do this by turning on worksheet protection prior to saving the workbook. Once done, you are assured that the spreadsheets generated from the template inherit the same level and type of protection that you did on the original spreadsheet.

Changing the Locked and Hidden protection formatting

There are ways to change the status of cells from locked to unlocked, or from hidden to unhidden, and you can find these on the check boxes at the Protection tab (Ctrl+1).

To remove the Locked protection status from a cell range, follow these steps:

1. Select the range of cells to be unlocked by holding down the Ctrl key and dragging the mouse pointer through each range.

2. Click the Format command button on the Home tab and click the Lock option at the bottom of the drop-down menu or press Alt+HOL.

Once you have all the cell ranges to be unlocked/locked or hidden/unhidden correctly, then it's time to turn on worksheet protection. Just click Protect Sheet on the Review tab, or press Alt+RPS to open the Protect Sheet dialog box.

Protecting the Workbook

The last level of protection that you can make on your spreadsheet is by protecting the whole workbook. When you protect your workbook, your users are not able to change anything on the file. You can do this by clicking the Protect

Workbook command on the Review tab and then choose Protect Structure or Alt+RPW. Excel then prevents you or your users from doing any of the following tasks to the file:

- Inserting new worksheets

- Delete existing sheets

- Rename sheets

- Hiding or viewing hidden sheets

- Moving or copying worksheets to a new workbook

- Displaying source data for a cell in a pivot table or showing a table's Report Filter fields

- Creating a summary report with the Scenario Manager

When you turn on the protection options for a workbook, Excel prevents you from changing the size or position of the workbook's windows. You can turn it off too, by choosing Protect Structure and Windows option on the Unprotect Workbook button, or by pressing Alt+RPW.

Chapter 12

Hyperlinks

What to expect from this chapter?

- The Basics of Hyperlinks
- How to Use the Hyperlink Function

In Excel, you can create hyperlinks that bring you do a different part of the same worksheet, another worksheet, to another workbook, or another type of document, as well as to a web page on the internet or the intranet.

The Basics of Hyperlinks

When adding hyperlinks on an Excel worksheet, you should first define two things:

- The object you want to anchor the link and then click to activate

- The destination to which the link takes you when activated

The destinations that you may specify for links can be new cell or cell range, the same workbook file, or another file outside of the workbook. Meanwhile, the destinations that you can specify for hyperlinks that take you to another place include:

- The cell reference of a cell in any of the worksheets on your workbook

- Range name of the group of cells in the worksheet or workbook

- The filename of an existing workbook file you want to open when clicking the hyperlink

- The URL of a webpage that you want to visit when clicking the hyperlink

- An email address for a new message that you want to create on the email app when you click the hyperlink.

Adding hyperlinks

To add a hyperlink to the text within a cell or a graphic object, you may do the following steps:

1. Put the cell pointer in the cell containing the text, or click the graphic object to which you want to anchor the hyperlink.

2. Click the Hyperlink command on the Insert tab or press Ctrl+K.

3. Type in the text that you want to appear next to the pointer in the Set Hyperlink dialog box, then click OK.

4. Choose the type of destination for the new link by clicking its button in the Link To panel at the Insert Hyperlink dialog box.

Once done, you need to specify the destination for the link. Doing this depends on the type of link that you are adding. Setting the destination varies on the following factors:

- Linking to a cell or range in the current workbook – after clicking Place in This Document, type in the address of the cell to link to in the Type the Cell Reference text box, then click the name of the sheet that contains this cell listed under the Cell Reference range, or Select a Place in This Document list box.

- Linking to an existing file – click the Existing File or Web Page button, open the folder in the Look In drop-down menu, then click the file icon in the list that appears below the box. If you are linking to a web page, click the Address text box and type in the URL of the address. If the file that choose has bookmarks that name specific locations in the file to which you link, click the Bookmark button and click the location in the Select Place in Document dialog box then click OK.

- Creating a new email message – Click the E-Mail Address button, then enter the email address in the text box, then click the Subject text box and type in the subject of the email message.

You can then specify the destination for the hyperlink using the text boxes and list boxes shown for the type of link destination that you have made. Once done, click the OK button in the Insert Hyperlink dialog box.

Using the HYPERLINK Function

Aside from using the Hyperlink command, you may also use Excel's HYPERLINK function to create a hypertext link. This function uses the following syntax:

HYPERLINK*(link_location[friendly_name])*

The link_location argument shows the name of the document to open on your local drive, or on a network server, company intranet, or the internet. The optional friendly_name argument is the hyperlink text that appear in the cell where you place the HYPERLINK FUNCTION.

When you omit this argument, Excel shows the text specified as the link_location argument in the cell.

Chapter 13

How to Prepare
a Workbook for Distribution

What to expect from this chapter?

- Readying for Review
- Annotations

In this chapter, you will learn how to check your workbook so that it becomes ready for distribution. You will find out how to annotate a spreadsheet with text notes to indicate comments, improvements, corrections, and highlight potential areas of change with ink.

Prepping for Review

The Info screen at the Backstage view (Alt+FI) allows you to ready your workbook for distribution by checking the properties of the workbook. In order to do this, just click the Check for Issues button at the Info screen then select any of the options below:

- Inspect Document – checks documents for hidden content and metadata. You can delete such content that you find before distributing the file by hitting the Remove All button.

- Check Accessibility – to make Excel scan the whole workbook file for information that people with specific disabilities might have difficulty with.

- Check Compatibility – checks a workbook file saved with the Excel Workbook XML format option for any loss in fidelity when it is saved in older workbook file formats.

The Info screen also contains a Manage Workbook button, which gives you two options for recovering draft versions of the workbook so that the final version will be the only one available for sharing:

- Check out – to edit a private copy of the workbook and disallow others to make changes on it

- Recover Unsaved Versions – to enable you go through all the versions of the workbook that were closed without saving the final changes using AutoRecover.

You will also find the Browser View Options button which opens the Browser View Options dialog box that features a Show and Parameters tab. This allows you to control which parts of the workbook are shown and can be edited when the file is shared online.

Adding properties to your workbook

You can add certain information about your workbook document on the Info panel in the Backstage view, and you can access this by going to File -> Info or Alt+FI. From there, you can use the metadata to enter information into the Title, Tags, Categories, and Author fields in the Info panel.

By doing this, you are able to quickly locate the file for opening in Excel for editing, printing, or distributing to others for review in the future.

When entering more than one piece of data into a certain field, separate each piece with a comma. Also, when you are done adding the metadata, close the Info panel by clicking the File menu at the top of the panel or by hitting Esc.

Adding a digital signature

Excel 2019 allows you to add a digital signature to your workbook files that you opt to send for review. After goring through the spreadsheet for accuracy and readiness for distribution, you can digitally sign the workbook in either of two ways:

- Add a signature line as a graphic object on the workbook that contains your name, signature date, title, and an inked handwritten signature (in case you are on a touchscreen device).

- Add an invisible signature as indicated by the Digital Signature icon on the status bar.

By doing this, you provide three things about your Excel workbook:

- Authenticity

- Integrity

- Nonrepudiation

In order to establish these assurances, your digital signature should be valid in the following ways:

- The certificate associated with the signature should be issued by a reputable certificate authority.

- The certificate should be valid.

- The signing publisher should be deemed trustworthy.

To add your digital signature, follow these steps:

1. Inspect the worksheet data and save all the final changes made on the workbook file. Then position the cell pointer in a blank cell where you want the signature line to appear.

2. Click Insert -> Add a Signature Line -> Microsoft Office Signature Line in the text group or Alt+NG.

3. Enter the signer's name on the Suggested Signer text box then press Tab.

4. Type the signer's title on the signer's title box, then press Tab.

5. Type the signer's email address on the signer's email address text box.

6. Click OK to close the Signature Setup.

Excel then adds a signature line graphic object in the area of the cell cursor with a big X that has your name and title.

Annotations

You may also annotate your worksheet by adding comments to the cells of a workbook, in particular those that seek clarification or changes. This helps when you are asking for specific feedback from those who will review your report.

Excel has made it easier to annotate the cells by having specific commands on the Review tab for you to use.

Adding comments

You can add comments to the workbook by clicking New Comment on a current cell or by pressing Alt+RC. Excel then responds by adding a Comment box with your name. You then start typing your comment. Once finished, click the cell to which you are attaching the note to close the Comment box.

Showing and hiding comments

Excel has the ability to indicate that you have attached a comment to a cell by adding a red triangle to that cell's upper right corner. You can then position the thick, white cross mouse pointer on this red triangle to display the Comment box, or click Show All Comments on the Review tab.

Editing and formatting comments

When you add a comment, the Comment box appears to the right of the cell with an arrow pointing to the red triangle. You may reposition a cell's Comment box or resize it so it does not get in the way of other cells in the surrounding region. You can also edit the text of a comment or modify the formatting of the text font.

To reposition or resize a Comment box, make the cell current by putting the cursor in it and then click Edit Comment, or Alt+RT.

Deleting comments

When you don't need comments anymore, you can delete them by selecting their cells, and then do any of the following:

- Choose the Comments option from the Clear drop-down menu, or Alt+HEM.

- Click the Delete command in the Comments group or press Alt+RD.

Marking up with digital ink

You can also mark up your worksheets using digital ink if you have a computer connected to a touchscreen device. You can do this by using commands on the Draw tab of the Ribbon.

Excel chooses the felt tip pen as the type for annotations using digital ink. You can change this if you prefer using a ballpoint pen or a highlighter. If you don't have a stylus available, you can tap the Draw with Touch command, then use your finger to make the annotations.

Once you have selected the pen nib, color, and line weight for your markup, you can use your finger or stylus to mark up the worksheet in ways such as:

- Highlight data in the spreadsheet with highlighter by dragging the moue pointer through the cells

- Circle data in the spreadsheet by dragging the pen tip mouse painter around the cells in your worksheet.

- Add a comment using a ballpoint pen by dragging the pen tip to write your text in the worksheet.

Chapter 14

Sharing Your Workbook and Worksheet

What to expect from this chapter?

- Sharing Workbooks Online
- Data Sharing Basics
- Exporting to Other Usable File Formats

Sharing data between Excel and other programs happens every now and then, especially when you are assigned to write reports for your company. The most common way to share worksheet data is by sharing the workbook on your OneDrive, SharePoint team site, or in a folder in Dropbox.

However, data is also shared by getting the Excel data placed in tables, lists, and charts into other Office 2019 programs, such as Microsoft Word and PowerPoint. There are also instances when you share data by means of generating data from other sources and placed into an Excel worksheet.

Sharing Workbooks Online

One of the perks of Excel 2019 is that it makes it easier for you to share spreadsheets online. You can use the options on the Share screen at the Backstage view to email your worksheets or send them via Skype to those who have Excel on their computers. In addition, you can also share workbooks saved on OneDrive or SharePoint for other users to access in their own devices or on web browsers via Excel Online.

This process is called co-authoring, and it enables you to see through all the people with whom you have shared a workbook as well as the editing changes that they make to it.

Sharing workbooks via OneDrive

To share Excel workbooks from OneDrive, simply follow these steps:

1. Open the workbook that you want to share on Excel 2019 then click the Share button at the far right of the row.

2. Type the email address of the person you want to share the workbook with.

3. Click the Anyone with the Link Can Edit button to go to the Link Settings dialog. Here you can make changes to the people for whom the link works, restrict editing privileges to those with whom you share the file, or set

expiration dates after which the link is no longer operational. Then click Apply.

4. Click Add a Message and type your personal message that you want to send as part of the email with the generic invitation to share the file.

5. Once you have added all the recipients of the link, click Share. Excel then emails the invite to each of the recipients that you entered in the Type Name or Email Addresses text box.

All the people whom you shared the workbook with will receive an email containing the hyperlink to the workbook on your OneDrive. When they follow the link, a copy of the workbook opens on a new page in their web browser, for them to view or edit, depending on the user permission you have provided to them.

Commenting

There are times when you need to share workbooks to different clients or co-workers who need to give you feedback about their worksheet data. In these situations, you can use Excel's Send Adobe PDF For Shared Commenting command that converts an Excel workbook into PDF format that can be shared on the same internal server or as an email attachment for them to review and comment via Adobe Acrobat software.

Once they make their comments on the PDF file, they can share or send a copy of the worksheet in PDF format or even have it converted into an Excel file. To send your workbook as a PDF, you can follow these steps:

1. Open the workbook file.

2. Click File -> Save as Adobe PDF to open Acrobat PDFMaker.

3. Select your Conversion Range and Conversion Options in the Acrobat PDFMaker dialog box, then click Convert to PDF.

4. Click save.

You may then review the PDF file in Acrobat, and if everything is set to go, you may decide how to share the file to your colleagues. Among your options are:

- Save File to Adobe Document Cloud – all co-workers with access to this services may open the file for review and annotations.

- Attach as Email – send the PDF file as a standard email attachment.

- Send & Track – send the link to co-workers via a default email app that allows them to preview the PDF file online.

Editing worksheets via Excel Online

You can also use Excel Online to edit worksheets that are saved on your OneDrive within your web browser. This proves to be handy especially when you don't have Excel installed on your computer or touchscreen device (if you are using someone else's device), as you can still make edits so long as you have an internet connection and a web browser that supports Excel Online.

To edit your workbook via Excel online, here are the steps to follow:

1. Launch the web browser that supports Excel Online then go to www.office.live.com and sign in to your Windows account.

2. Once logged in, Click the Excel button. There you will see a series of thumbnails, starting with the New Blank Workbook. You will also see the following options when selecting a file to edit, such as: Recent, Pinned, Shared with Me, Discover, and Upload and Open.

3. Find the Excel workbook that you want to edit then click its filename, and start editing.

4. Once done, click Close. You may save a copy of the workbook under a new filename in the same folder on OneDrive by clicking File -> Save As then edit the

filename that appears in the text box before you click the Save button.

Basics of Excel 2019 Data Sharing

you may share information between Excel and other programs by either copying or moving discrete objects of data from one program's file to another (and vice versa), or open a new file created with one program in the other program.

When sharing blocks of data in Excel, you make use of the Windows Clipboard. Excel allows you access to Clipboard contents in the form of the Clipboard task pane, where you can open by clicking the Dialog Box launcher found in the Clipboard group. Once the Clipboard task pane is open, you may copy its contents into the cells of an open worksheet.

It is also worth noting that Microsoft offers you options to exchange data between different Office programs. You may do so by:

- Embedding – the Excel object becomes part of the Word document or PowerPoint slideshow. The changes you need to make to the worksheet should be made within the Word or PowerPoint file.

- Linking – the Excel object is only referred to in the Word document or PowerPoint presentation. Changes made to the worksheet or chart must be done on Excel then updated when you open Word or PowerPoint to which the data is linked.

Exporting Workbooks to Different Usable File Formats

There are also instances when you have to share worksheet data with other people who do not have Excel on their computers or devices. In this regard, they cannot open or print the Excel workbook file you send them, so you can export your workbook to either of these usable file formats for opening and printing:

- PDF files for opening with Adobe Reader or Adobe Acrobat

- XPS files for opening using XML Paper Specification Viewer

- ODS files for opening with open source spreadsheet programs

- HTML files for opening with all types of web browsers.

When converting an Excel workbook to one of these formats, you may change the file type in the Save As dialog box, or export them from the Export screen via File -> Export.

Saving worksheets as PDF files

One of the most common file formats to which workbooks are converted to is the PDF. It enables people to open, view, and print documents without accessing or modifying the original programs from which they were created.

Excel 2019 allows you to save your workbook directly as PDF. To do this, click File -> Save As (Alt+FA), then select where you want to save the new PDF file, and then select PDF from the Save as Type drop-down menu.

Saving worksheets as XPS

Another format in which workbooks can be saved is via XPS (XML Paper Specification). It also enables you to open and print the worksheet without access to the program itself. It can be opened by anyone on Internet Explorer 10, or through its earlier versions that has an XPS Viewer installed.

Just like the PDF format, you can convert your worksheets to XPS by following the same procedure as above, but instead of choosing PDF for file type, choose XPS. You may also select Publish on the Save As dialog and choose Publish as XPS.

Saving as ODS

ODS (OpenDocument Spreadsheet) is the spreadsheet file format being used by OpenOffice.org's Calc program. To save in this format, choose OpenDocument Spreadsheet (*.ods) option of the Save as Type menu.

Saving as HTML

You may also save your worksheets via HTML, as this enables everybody to view and print the spreadsheet file via any browser. To save in this format, go to Click File -> Save AS, then choose the drive and folder where you intend to save the web version of the workbook, then choose Single File Web Page or Web Page at the Save as Type menu.

You may choose Single File Web Page if the workbook only has one spreadsheet, or if you want your data on all worksheets appear on a single page. When you select either option, Excel expands the Save As dialog to include Entire Workbook and Selection.

Then give your web page a new filename in the File Name text box. Excel automatically appends the filename extension .htm to whatever filename you want to enter. When choosing a filename, do note that some file servers are sensitive to upper and lowercase letters in the said name.

Afterwards, enter the filename for the new HTML file in the File Name text box.

You may also do some more tweaks, such as selecting the Sheet option button if you just want to save the current worksheet into the new HTML file.

PART 5:

Graphics and Charts

Chapter 15

Charting Your Worksheet Data

What to expect from this chapter?

- The Basics of Worksheet Charting
- Adding Sparkline Graphics
- Adding Infographics
- Printing Charts

Charts showcase data on your worksheet in a visual manner, by representing columns and rows as bars on a chart or graph. Charts and graphs have been part of spreadsheets because they enable you to see patterns that you can't easily see from the numbers per se.

In this chapter, you will be acquainted with the jargon used in Excel to refer to the parts of the chart, such as data marker and chart data series, as well as axis. Getting acquainted with these terms is important as they guide you through the simple steps needed to create the graph or chart that you want.

The Basics of Worksheet Charting

The Excel chart is made up of different parts. These include:

- Chart area – all the space inside the chart window, including all parts of the chart.

- Data marker – a symbol that represents a single value in the spreadsheet

- Chart data series – a group of related values in a single row in the chart

- Series formula – a formal that describes the given series, including a reference to the cell that has the data series information.

- Axis – it is the line that acts as a major reference for plotting data on the chart.

- Tick mark – a small line that intersects an axis.

- Plot area – the area wherein Excel plots the data, including the axes and markers that represent data points

- Gridlines – lines extending from the tick marks across the plot area

- Chart text – a label added to the chart

- Legend – the key that names patterns, colors, or symbols linked to the markers of a chart data series

Adding recommended charts

One of the easiest ways to add a chart on your spreadsheet is by using the Recommended Charts that can be found on the Insert tab (Alt+NR). In this tab, you can see how the selected worksheet data will be represented in different chart types by simply clicking their thumbnails. Once you have chosen a chart type, just click the OK button to embed it on your worksheet.

Adding specific chart types

Aside from Recommended Charts, you may also use different styles of charts, such as:

- Column or Bar Chart

- Hierarchy Chart

- Waterfall, Funnel, Stock, Surface, or Radar Chart

- Line or Area Chart

- Statistic Chart

- Combo Chart

- Pie or Doughnut Chart

- Scatter (X, Y) or Bubble Chart

- Maps

- PivotChart

When using the galleries linked to these chart commands, you may embed the chart in your worksheet by clicking its corresponding icon. If you are not sure of the kind of chart that best represents your data, then you may use the All Charts tab to try out your data in different chart representations.

Editing your chart's source data

There are times when you need to edit the data of your chart, and you can do this by clicking Select Data on the Design tab of the Chart Tools. Excel then opens the Select Data Source dialog box and this enables you to make the following modifications:

- Modify the range of data being graphed

- Switch column and row headings

- Edit labels that identify the data series in the legend

- Add an additional data series to the chart

- Remove a label from the legend

- Change the order of the data series

- Show how to deal with empty cells in the data range

- Show data in Hidden Rows and Columns

Adding Sparkline Graphics

Excel 2019 has a feature called "sparklines," which show trends or variations in your collected data. These are tiny graphs whose data can be any of the following chart types:

- Line – represents chosen worksheet data as a connected line whose vectors show their relative value

- Column – represents selected worksheet data as small columns

- Win/Loss – represents the selected worksheet data as a win/loss chart

You can add sparklines to your worksheet by doing the following steps:

1. Choose the cells with the data you want to be represented by a sparkline.

2. Click the type of chart you want for the sparkline in the Sparklines group at the Insert Tab or press Alt+NSL for line, Alt+NSO for column, or Alt+NSW for win/loss.

3. Choose the cell or range of cells where you want to add your sparkline in the Location Range text box, then click OK to close.

Adding Infographics

Aside from graphs, Excel 2019 also allows you to add infographics to your worksheet via the Bing Maps and People Graph at the drop-down menu of the Insert Tab's Add-Ins button. These infographics enhancements allow you to create visual representations of worksheet data that is based on regions, and point out trends that quickly show their most pertinent information.

In order to do this, you need geographically-related data. Excel recognizes certain geographic regions automatically, and these include:

- Names of countries, such as USA, Canada, China, etc.

- Names of provinces, such as Ontario, Ontario, Manitoba, etc.

- Names of states, such as California, Florida, New Mexico, etc.

- Two-letter state abbreviations, such as NY, MD, CA

- Postal codes such as 90210, 44135, WC2N 5DU

Printing Charts

When printing an embedded chart, you simply go to the Print Settings screen or press Ctrl+P. To print the chart without the supporting data, click the chart to select it before pressing Ctrl+P. In the Print Selected Chart you will see a default selection in the first drop-down menu, and a preview of the chart appears in the Preview pane on the right of the screen.

To print a chart that is on a separate chart sheet, activate the chart sheet by clicking its sheet tab and then press Ctrl+P to go to the Print panel, then choose Print Active Sheet in order to print the said chart.

Chapter 16

Adding Graphic Objects

What to expect from this chapter?

- Basics of Graphic Objects
- Inserting Different Graphic Types and Forms
- Drawing Graphic Objects
- Adding Screenshots
- Using Themes

While charts can help clarify trends, graphics meanwhile can be useful in bringing more life to your worksheet data. You not only get to use them as enhancements, but you may also utilize them to boost regular data.

Excel 2019 supports two different types of graphic objects, those that you create on your own and those that you import from other sources.

Basics of Graphic Objects

All graphic objects, regardless if you create them or import them, are discrete objects in the worksheet that you can manipulate. To select a graphic object, you just click it. From there, Excel lets you know that the object is selected and how it can be controlled.

Meanwhile, in order to select multiple graphic objects, hold the Shift or Ctrl key once you click each object. To deselect, just click the white cross pointer in any cell on the worksheet that the graphic object does not occupy.

Controlling graphics

When working with objects, the mouse pointer becomes a double-headed arrow in which you can drag to increase or decrease the object's overall size and shape. You may also constrain a graphic while resizing it, by clicking the sizing handle and then pressing and holding down the Shift key as you drag.

When you place the pointer on an object's 2-D or 3-D rotation handle, the pointer becomes a curved arrow that points clockwise. When you prepare to drag the 2-D rotation handle, the pointer becomes four curved arrows in a circle that points to the clockwise direction. From there you can rotate the graphic to any degree that pivots around the rotation handle.

Meanwhile, when you position the pointer in an object's 3-D rotation handle, the pointer becomes a circular arrow, also pointing clockwise. You can then rotate the object in a 3-dimensional space so that the object can be displayed from any angle above, below, in front, at the back, or on either side.

To move the graphics object, place the mouse pointer in the object's perimeter. When the pointer becomes an arrowhead, drag the object to its new position within the worksheet.

To copy the selected object, just hold down the Ctrl key while dragging the graphic.

When working with a graphic object on a touchscreen device, use your finger or stylus on the different handles to rotate, resize, or reshape the image.

Moving graphic objects to different layers

You can also do layering on graphic objects in your worksheet. This means, if you move a graphic object over a cell that has an entry, the graphic hides the data beneath it, or vice versa.

Excel allows you to move graphic objects on the worksheet to different layers using the Selection task pane. Just click the name of the object that you want to move and drag the object up or down in the task pane. You can also use the Bring Forward button or Send Backward button to move the object.

Different Types of Graphics

Excel allows for different types of graphics to be used on worksheets, and they can be further utilized using the options in the Illustration button of the Insert tab. These include:

- Pictures

- Online pictures

- Shapes

- Icons

- 3D Models

- SmartArt

- Screenshot

How to insert 2-D online images

If you need to insert 2-D online images, you can go to the Online Pictures dialog box or Alt+NF, then choose one of the categories displayed or choose the Select Bing text box to type the keyword for the images you want to use.

After doing a search, the Online Pictures dialog box shows a scrollable list of images that match your keyword. You can then point the mouse on any of the thumbnails to see their descriptions and sizes.

To download images on saved on OneDrive, click the Browse button to the right of the Bing heading then click OneDrive on the drop-down menu. Excel will display a list of folders that you can open and get the image that you want to place on your worksheet.

How to insert 3-D online images

You can also insert 3-D online images by choosing the 3D Models command at the Illustrations group of the Insert tab (Alt+NS30). To do so, open the said dialog box and choose a thumbnail of the model from one of the displayed categories or from a search that you make of the 3-D images.

Inserting local images

You may also want to insert an image such as a digital photo or a scanned image that's locally saved on your computer onto your worksheet. You can do this by choosing the Pictures option from the Illustration's dropdown menu, or press Alt+NP.

Editing images

You can edit your images through the following steps:

- To move an image, drag it with your mouse pointer.

- To resize, select the image then drag the sizing handle.

- To rotate, select the image then drag its rotation handle in a clockwise or counter-clockwise direction.

Drawing Graphic Objects

You can also draw shapes using SmartArt, TextBox, and WordArt on Excel.

Drawing shapes

You can start drawing shapes by going to the Shapes gallery, then choose a wide array of predefined shapes by dragging the mouse pointer to a thumbnail of your chosen shape. Afterwards, click the thumbnail of the preset shape, then use the mouse pointer to draw the graphic by dragging it on the worksheet until it becomes the size that you want.

Adding text boxes

Text boxes meanwhile are special graphic objects that combine text with a graphic object. They are useful in calling attention to certain trends and features on the charts that you make.

To make a text box, click the Text Box button in the Insert tab (Alt+ NX). Then drag the pointer's cursor to the outline of the new text box. When you release the mouse button, Excel draws the text box and place an insertion point where you can start typing the text that you want displayed.

WordArt

You can also make your presentation text quirky via the WordArt command. You can do this by:

1. Click the WordArt button or Alt+NW

2. Click a thumbnail in the WordArt style that you want to use.

3. Type the text that you want to be seen on the worksheet in the text box.

4. To format the text box's background, use Live Preview in the Shape Styles drop-down and find the style that you want to use.

5. After making final adjustments to size, shape, or orientation of the WordArt text, click a cell outside of the text to deselect the WordArt graphic.

SmartArt Graphics

SmartArt graphics allow you to construct fancy diagrams and captioned pictures on your worksheet. To insert a SmartArt graphic, click the SmartArt button or Alt+M1, then choose a category located in the navigation pane on the left, followed by the thumbnail of the SmartArt graphic that you want to use, then click OK.

Adding Screenshots

You may also add screenshots on your worksheet via the Screenshot button. However, before you use this command, you have to open up another application window whose document you wish to capture as an Excel graphic object.

When you have application windows open on the Windows desktop, a thumbnail of these windows will show on the Screenshot drop-down menu under the heading Available Screen Shots. To capture an open window's information as a graphic object, click its thumbnail on the drop-down list and Excel then adds the window as a graphic object on your worksheet.

Themes

Excel 2019 also allows you to format the graphics that you add on your worksheet. You can choose a new theme for the active worksheet by clicking the thumbnail of the theme you intend to use in the Themes drop-down gallery or Alt+PTH.

Excel Themes has three default elements: color scheme, the font, and the graphic effects applied. You can change any or all these elements in the worksheet by clicking on their individual buttons at the Themes group at the start of the Page Layout tab.

PART 6:

Managing Data

Chapter 17

Building Data Lists

What to expect from this chapter?

- Basics of Data Lists
- Data Sorting
- Subtotalling Your Data

A side from its computational functions, Excel is also known for maintaining vast collections of related data called database tables or data lists. These are tables of worksheet data that uses a special structure called field names to identify different kinds of items on its list tracks.

Each column in the data list has information for each item you track, from dates to company names to phone numbers. Meanwhile, each row in the data list has complete information about each entity you track on the data list, known as record.

The Basics of Data Lists

Data lists follow a structure that you can set up with a wide range of commands found on the Data tab. It is important to get to know these tools especially when you are maintaining data. You must know how to reorder the information it contains without damaging its integrity.

Designing a data list

When designing a data list, all you have to do is enter the names of the fields that you want to track on the top row of the worksheet. Afterwards, enter the record of data underneath each field, then format the two rows of data as a table.

When entering field names, note that each name in the list is unique, so keep them short. You may likewise align the field name in the cell so that its text wraps to a new line via the Wrap Text command button. It is also worth noting not to use numbers or formulas that show values as field names.

To set up your data list, here are the following steps:

1. Click the blank cell where you want to begin the new data list and then enter the field names that identify the items that you need to keep track of.

2. Make the first entries in the appropriate columns of the row below the one that has the field names.

3. Click Format as Table, then click a thumbnail of one of the styles in the drop-down list.

4. Click OK to close.

Adding records to a data list

Once you have created the field names and one record of the data list and formatted them as a table, you can start entering other records in the succeeding rows. The easiest way to do this is by pressing the Tab key when the cursor is the in last cell of the first record.

Eliminating duplicates

You may also remove duplicates in your records by using the Eliminate Duplicates feature, especially when you are dealing with a large data list with several people doing the data entry and should not have duplicate records.

To remove duplicate records from a data list, follow these steps:

1. Position the cursor in one of the cells in the data list.

2. Click the Remove Duplicates button on the Data tab or press Alt+AM.

3. Remove all the check marks from the fields in the Columns list box save for those whose duplicates are reason for removing the record.

4. Click OK to close the Remove Duplicates dialog and remove the duplicate records from the selected list.

Data Sorting

After building and filling up a data list, you can sort records in your data list. You can specify an ascending or descending sort order, as well as other options available on the Sort drop-down list.

When you specify ascending order, Excel arranges the text in an A-Z order and values from smallest to biggest. Meanwhile, if you specify descending order, Excel reverses the order and arranges the text from Z-A and values from largest to smallest.

You may also sort on a date field, but keep in mind that the ascending order puts the records in oldest to newest order, while descending order gives records in newest to oldest date order.

Subtotalling Your Data

You may also use the Subtotals feature to subtotal data in your sorted data list. When doing so, you sort the list on the field where you want subtotals to be shown before you assign the field that contains the values you want subtotalled, as these are not always the same fields in your data list.

Do note that when you use this feature, you are not restricted to having the values in the assigned field to be added with the SUM function. Rather, you can make Excel return the number of entries using the COUNT function, the average of the entries via the AVERAGE function, the highest entry with MAXIMUM function, the lost with the MINIMUM function, and the product of the entries using the PRODUCT function.

Chapter 18

Filters and Queries

What to expect from this chapter?

- What You Need to Know About Data List Filtering
- Filtering Data
- Using Database Functions
- External Data Query
- A Quick Mention on Macros and VBA

Aside from building a data list from scratch, you also have to learn how to get specific information that you need from that list. Extracting data is important and on Excel, it can be done via filtering and querying procedures.

Excel has Database functions that perform calculations based on the criteria that you specify, such as getting totals (DSUM), averages (DAVERAGE), count of records (DCOUNT and DCOUNTA), etc.

Data List Filtering

When working on data lists, you will encounter vast quantity of stored data. However, it should not be confused with information that particular people in your organization want out of the data. This is because data only represent numbers and texts, but it is in the way they are interpreted that they become information.

For most people, a data list dispenses information only when you are able to filter stuff that you don't want to see, and it leaves behind only data that can be interpreted into information that concerns them.

Filtering Data

Excel allows you to filter your data list so it shows only information that you want to work with. You can do this via the AutoFilter feature, which temporarily hides the display of records you don't want to see and leaves only the records that you are going to use.

There are times however, when the AutoFilter feature is not enough so you can do advanced filtering on your data list, especially when you are using computed criteria.

AutoFilter

Excel's AutoFilter feature allows filtering easier. You can do this by clicking the AutoFilter button on the column that you want to filter data and then choosing the filtering criteria from that column's drop-down list.

If your worksheet data list has no AutoFilter buttons to each of the field names, you can display them by positioning the cell pointer in one of the cells with the filed names then click the Filter button on the Data Tab or Ctrl+Shift+L.

Basic Filtering

The AutoFilter drop-down menu has a list box that contains all entries made in that column, together with their own checkboxes. You can filter the data list by clearing the check box for the entries whose records you don't want to see. You can do this by deselecting the check box in front of the option at the top of the field's list box to clear the check boxes, then choose each of the boxes containing the entries for the records you want to be shown.

Once done, click OK to close the AutoFilter drop-down list.

Database Functions

Excel also has a number of database functions that you may use to compute for things such as statistics, like the total, average, maximum, and minimum, and count in a certain field of the data list based on criteria you specify to be met.

Regardless of the difference in names, database functions take only three arguments, as shown by the DAVERAGE function:

$$DAVERAGE(database, field, criteria)$$

The arguments for database functions are:

- Database – argument that specifies the range containing the list and must include the row of field names on the top row

- Field – argument that specifies the field where the values are to be computed by the database function.

- Criteria – the argument that specifies the address of the range that has the criteria you are using to determine which values are calculated.

Database functions are rarely used to rate their own command button in the Formulas tab, so in order to use them in a worksheet, click the Insert Function (fx) button on the Formula bar, then choose Database from the Select a Category drop-down list, and click the function to use or type the Database function directly into the cell.

External Data Query

Excel 2019 also makes it easier to query data lists stored in other databases that you need to extract for further manipulation and analysis. These data sources include Microsoft Access database files, web pages, text files, and tables on SQL Servers and Analysis Services, XML data, and data tables from online connections to Windows Azure and OData Data feeds.

When importing data from external sources, you may also be dealing with data stored in several related tables in the database, referred to as a Data Model. The link between these tables in the same database is based on a common field that occurs in each related data table that is known as a key field known as a lookup column.

When relating tables on a common key field, the records for that field should be unique with no duplicates (known as primary key). In the other related data table, the common field, known as the foreign key, may or not be unique.

There are two relationships supported by the Excel Data Model:

- One-to-one relationship –entries in both primary and foreign key fields are unique

- One-to-many relationship –duplicate entries in the foreign key field are allowed

Excel 2019 can figure out the relationship between the data tables you import, but if ever Excel gets it wrong, you can define the right relationship properly. Just choose the Relationships button in the Data Tools group of the Data Tab or Alt+AZDA.

To import data from an external database, you select Get Data or Alt+APN, and then choose between the following options:

- From File

- From Database

- From Azure

- From Online Services

- From Other Sources

- From Text/CSV

Data query in the Power Query Editor

Whenever you conduct a data query in Excel 2019 using the Get Data command, you have the option of transforming that query in the Power Query Editor. You do this by opening the Power Query Editor after specifying the data table/s to import into excel by clicking the Transform Data in the Navigator dialog box.

Do note that when you use the Table/Range command to assign a selected cell range as a data table, Excel opens the data table in a new Power Query Editor window so you can create or transform an existing query.

Automating Tasks via Macros

In Excel, you can automate your tasks by using macros. Excel has a macro recorder to document and run tasks that you run on a regular basis, in order to speed up your work and assure you that each step is carried out in the same manner each and every time you do the task. Macros record all commands, keystrokes, and mouse actions that you do for the task via a language called Visual Basic for Applications or VBA.

Basics of Macros

You can create macros by using the macro recorder on Excel, or by entering the instructions that you want followed in VBA code via the Visual Basic Editor.

Excel creates a special module sheet that contains all the actions in your macro and are stored in Visual Basic for Applications programming language. You can then play with the code on the macro recorder which is found in the Developer tab or Alt+F11.

Using the Visual Basic Editor

The Visual Basic Editor is always ready for use, and you can find it when you press Alt+F11. When accessing the Visual Basic Editor, you can then study, record, and run macros and modify them based on your needs.

PART 7:

Analyzing Data

Chapter 19

What-if Scenarios

What to expect from this chapter?

- Data Tables
- Exploring Different Scenarios
- Hide and Goal Seeking
- Using the Solver

One of the wonderful things in Excel is that it allows you to do electronic fortune telling via the What-if Scenarios. A what-fi analysis, while just an assumption, provides you with a rather scientific view of a forecast, and not just based on a hunch or whim.

In Excel, a what-if analysis comes in a wide array of scenarios using three simple methods:

- Data tables – allow you to see how changing one or two variables affect the end result.

- Goal seeking – allows you to see what it takes to reach an objective

- Scenarios – allow you to set up and test different cases, all the way from the best to the worst case scenario.

Data Tables

In an Excel worksheet, you can see how changing an input value affects the result returned by a formula the moment you add a new input value in the cell that feeds into the formula. It automatically recalculates the formula and shows you a new result.

This method, while convenient, cannot always be used on a what-if analysis. Hence, to perform such task, you can go to Excel's Data Table command.

When Excel is finished computing the data table, you can see the results produced by the changes on the input values in a single range worksheet and save the data table as part of the worksheet.

If you want to see how using a different range of variables affects the results in the table, just enter the new input values in the existing page.

You may also click Automatic Except Data Tables (Alt+MXE) if you want to control when each data table is recalculated while at the same time allowing the formulas in the spreadsheet to be automatically recomputed.

Exploring Different Scenarios

Excel also allows you to come up with sets of input values that show different results called scenarios, using the Scenario Manager option in the What-If Analysis button's drop-down list.

A scenario is comprised of a group of input values to which you can assign as Best Case, Worst Case, Most Likely Case, etc.

To reuse the input data and see the results that they create in the worksheet, just select the name of the scenario that you want to use.

After creating different scenarios, you may also use the Scenario Manager to come up with a new summary report that shows both input values stored in each scenario and the key results they have produced.

Creating scenarios

To build a scenario using the Scenario Manager, take the following steps:

1. Choose the changing cells in the spreadsheet, cells whose values vary in every scenario.

2. Click the What-If Analysis command then go to Scenario Manager.

3. Click the Add button in the Scenario Manager dialog.

4. Add a name for the scenario in the Scenario Name text box.

5. Choose what kind of scenario protection you need in the Protection section of the Add Scenario dialog box.

6. Click OK.

7. Check the values in the changing cells' text box and tweak as necessary.

8. Click the Add button in Scenario Values.

9. Repeat steps 4-7 to bring in all other scenarios that you want to make.

10. Click OK then Close.

Creating a summary report

After creating scenarios for your worksheet, you can then use the Summary button in the Scenario Manager to come up with a summary report that presents the changing values used in the scenarios you've made.

At the Scenario Summary dialog box, you can designate a cell selection of result cells in the Result Cells section, so that these would be included in the report. After choosing the result cells, click OK to make Excel generate a report.

Hide and Goal Seeking

There are also times when you know the end result that you want to achieve in a worksheet, and you need Excel to help you find the input values to achieve such results. This is called goal seeking, the opposite of a what-if analysis.

This command is useful when you need to find the value for a single variable that will help you get the desired result of a particular formula. To use this command, just select the cell that contains the formula that will give the result that you are looking for (set cell), indicate the value you intend to get from the formula, and the location of the input value that Excel can modify to get the targeted result.

Using the Solver

While the Data Table and Goal Seek commands work for simple problems, you need to use the Solver add-in to deal with rather complex issues. This add-in is used to find the best solution when you have to make changes in multiple input values in your data model and you need to place constraints on these values and their output values.

The Solver add-in works by applying iterative methods to find the "best" way to solve the scenario. With each iteration, the program uses a trial-and-error method that tries to get closer and closer to the optimum solution.

To set up the problem for the Solver add-in, you need to define the following items:

- Objective cell – target cell in the worksheet whose value is to be made to reach a certain value.

- Variable cells – changing cells in the worksheet whose values are to be tweaked to get the answer.

- Constraint cells – cells that carry limits that you impose on the changing values.

Once you finish defining the problem with these parameters and run the Solver to fix the problem, the program provides the best solution by modifying the values in the worksheet. You can then choose to retain changes or restore original values, and have the solution as a scenario to view later on.

Chapter 20

Large Scale Data Analysis

What to expect from this chapter?

- Building Pivot Tables
- Modifying the Pivot Table
- Creating Pivot Charts
- Creating Forecast Worksheets

Analysing large scale data on your worksheet can be done using the pivot table and its pivot chart. These features enable you to summarize large amounts of data faster, thus revealing relationships, patterns and trends, and as well visualize these connections in just a few clicks.

Building Pivot Tables

A pivot table is a term given to a data summary table that you can use to reveal relationships in the data lists that you maintain in Excel. They are great for summarizing particular values in a database because through them you no longer need to create formulas to perform calculations.

Pivot tables allow you to play around with the arrangement of summarized data, even after you generate the table. Excel offers three ways to create pivot tables, via the Quick Analysis Tool, Recommended PivotTables button, and the Pivot Table button.

Creating a pivot table using the Quick Analysis tool

When using the Quick Analysis tool, you can preview various kinds of pivot tables in Excel by doing the following steps:

1. Choose all the data (including column headings) in your database as a cell range.

2. Click the Quick Analysis tool at the lower right corner of the cell selection.

3. Click the Tables tab.

4. To see each pivot table, highlight its PivotTable button in the Quick Analysis palette.

5. Once you have chosen a pivot table, click its thumbnail button to create it on your worksheet.

Using Recommended Pivot Tables

Another way to create a pivot table is via the Recommended Pivot Tables command. To use this method, here are the following steps:

1. Choose a cell in the database where you want to create the pivot table.

2. Click the Recommended PivotTables command on the Insert tab or Alt+NSP.

3. Select the sample of the pivot table that you want to build in the list box then click OK.

Manually creating pivot tables

You may also create pivot tables from scratch, and this is recommended when you want your pivot table to work on data from fields in more than one data table or when connecting with an external data source.

To create a pivot table using a data list in your Excel workbook, just open the worksheet that contains the list that you want summarized, place the pointer somewhere in the cells of the list, then click the PivotTable button. Excel then selects all the data in the list as covered by a marquee then opens a Create PivotTable dialog where you can make the necessary adjustments on the cell range to include/exclude data to be summarized.

To create a pivot table from external data, you may want to locate the cell pointer in the first cell of the worksheet where you want the pivot table to be created before clicking Create PivotTable. Once done, open the Create PivotTable dialog box where Excel selects the Use an External Data Source option and the Existing Worksheet option as the location for the new pivot table. To specify the external data table to use, click Choose Connections to open the Existing Connections dialog, where you can pick the connection you want to use. You can then play with the PivotTable Fields task pane, where you can add or remove data fields.

To complete the new pivot table, you have to assign the fields in the PivotTable Fields task pane to the other parts of the table by dragging a field name from the Choose Fields to Add to Report list box to any of the four areas in the Drag Fields Between Areas Below section.

Modifying the Pivot Table

You can modify your pivot table in accordance to your preferences or how you want the report to be presented. All you have to do is go to the PivotTable Fields task pane (Alt+JTL) to switch columns and rows to rearrange fields and values but still show the same totals.

Creating Pivot Charts

Aside from generating a pivot table, you can also spice up your data summaries by generating a pivot chart to represent your records and values. To do this, simply follow these steps:

1. Click the PivotChart button in the Tools group on the Analyze tab under the PivotTable Tools or press Alt+JTC.

2. Click the thumbnail of the chart that you want to create then click OK.

Once you click OK, Excel inserts a pivot chart into the worksheet that has the original pivot table. This chart contains drop-down buttons for each of the four fields used in the pivot chart and you can use them to filter and sort data based on the chart.

You may also move a pivot chart to a dedicated sheet by doing the following steps:

1. Click the Analyze tab under the PivotChart Tools tab.

2. Click New Sheet option in the Move Chart dialog box.

3. Rename the generic chart sheet name to your preferred name.

4. Click OK to close the Move Chart dialog box.

Creating Forecast Worksheets

You may also turn your worksheet that contains historical financial data into a visual forecast worksheet via the Forecast Worksheet feature. All you have to do is open the worksheet with historical data, position the cursor to one of its cells, then click the Forecast Sheet button found on the Data Tab or Alt+AFC.

Excel then selects all the historical data in the worksheet table while opening the Create Forecast Worksheet dialog box where you can make use of the following forecasting commands:

- Forecast Start – to select a starting data in the historical data

- Confidence Interval – to select a new degree of confidence for Excel to use in setting lower and upper confidence bound line

- Seasonally – choose between Detect Automatically to Set Manually

- Include Forecast Statistics – to show a table of forecast accuracy metrics

- Timeline Range – to modify cell range containing the date values in historical data

- Values Range – tweaks the cell range containing financial values in historical data

- Fill Missing Points Using – for Excel to fill in missing data points

Aggregate Duplicates Using – tweaks statistical functions.

Made in the USA
Middletown, DE
15 September 2019